POCKET REFERENCE

REPTILES
& Amphibians

A practical guide to over 180 of the most familiar British and European reptiles and amphibians described and illustrated in colour

Pamela Forey & Peter Forey

BROCKHAMPTON PRESS

CAUTION

 VENOMOUS SNAKES may bite if threatened. They have been given this warning symbol in the illustrations. If you have any doubt about the identity of a snake you encounter, we suggest you do not approach it (many of the non-venomous snakes will also bite hard if threatened and their bites are not pleasant, even if not life-threatening). Any snake bite can produce symptoms of shock, even if no venom has been injected.

Bites from most vipers swell if venom has been injected, and may induce sweating, giddiness and vomiting; they require medical attention as soon as possible. However, the venom will spread more rapidly if the bitten person moves about a lot. We suggest that you remain calm, move the affected area as little as possible, and get to a hospital quickly.

This edition published in 2000 by
Brockhampton Press,
20 Bloomsbury Street,
London WC1B 3QA,

This edition produced under licence by
Malcolm Saunders Publishing Ltd, London

© 1997 this edition Malcolm Saunders Publishing Ltd, London

All rights reserved. No part of this publication may be reproduced, stored in a retrieval system, or transmitted, in any form or by any means, electronic, mechanical, photocopying, recording or otherwise without the prior written permission of the copyright holder.

A CIP Catalogue record for this book is available from the British Library

Title: Pocket Reference Guides, REPTILES & AMPHIBIANS
ISBN: 1 86019 783 3

Printed in China by Colorcraft

Contents

INTRODUCTION	8
HOW TO USE THIS BOOK	8
GUIDE TO IDENTIFICATION	8
ILLUSTRATED GLOSSARY	12
BIOLOGY OF AMPHIBIANS	14
BIOLOGY OF REPTILES	16

Amphibians:	18-51
SALAMANDERS and NEWTS	**18**
FROGS and TOADS	**33**

Reptiles:	52-121
LIZARDS	**52**
WORM-LIZARDS	89
SNAKES	**90**
TORTOISES, TERRAPINS and TURTLES	**115**
INDEX	122

Introduction

We are used to seeing birds, insects and plants all around us, all the time. We take them for granted. But somehow spotting a lizard on a wall, or a having a toad in the garden is different. And snakes may add an element of danger, for although many are harmless, others will bite and a few are very dangerous.

This book is about the reptiles and amphibians of Europe, newts, toads, lizard, snakes and their relatives. It is written for those of you who would like to know more about these animals, but who know very little when you acquire this book. Its chief aim is to enable you to identify, as simply as possible, any which you are likely to find. It will also provide you with some idea of the lives that they lead, the places they can be found, and which to treat with caution.

How to use this book

The two groups of animals in this book, **amphibians** and **reptiles**, are quite different. There are six sections, two of amphibians (**Salamanders and Newts**, and **Frogs and Toads**) and four of Reptiles (**Lizards**, **Worm-lizards**, **Snakes**, and **Tortoises, Terrapins and Turtles**). Each section is indicated by a different colour band at the top of the page (see contents page). If you find an animal that you would like to identify, you first need to decide whether it is an amphibian or a reptile, and then to which section it belongs, using the information in the *Guide to identification*.

Guide to identification

First decide whether your animal is an amphibian or a reptile:

Amphibians

All amphibians have soft, permeable, usually moist, smooth skin with no scales (although toads may be rough and warty). All European species have four limbs, and their feet have no claws on their toes. Amphibians generally live in damp places or in water because they have little ability to tolerate desiccation, and most of them have to return to water to breed, usually in spring. Breeding ponds or streams in spring are therefore one of the best places to find amphibians.

SALAMANDERS & NEWTS (pages 18-32) are small, smooth-skinned amphibians with long bodies and long tails. All the European species have four more or less equal-sized legs. Many live in damp conditions or water, and these have moist skin; others live wholly or partly on land, and in these terrestrial animals the skin is more glossy or velvety.

FROGS & TOADS (pages 33-51) are also relatively small, but very different in shape. They have shortened bodies, long hind legs with more or less webbed toes, and shorter fore legs. Frogs, tree frogs and spadefoot toads have moist, relatively smooth skin, but true toads are drier, rougher, often warty animals.

Reptiles

All reptiles have dry, impermeable skin covered with horny scales. In some species, the scales are smooth, even glossy, and the animals look smooth in consequence; in others the scales are keeled, and the animals look and feel rough in texture. Some reptiles, like tortoises, also have a covering of bony plates. Reptiles with limbs have sharp claws on their toes; snakes and some lizards, however, lack limbs. Most reptiles live on land, in a wider variety of places than amphibians, because they can tolerate a wider variety of conditions; a few, like turtles, have returned to life in water. Reptiles are likely to be encountered in more or less any habitat, but although some are relatively large and obvious, many others are small, fast-moving and/or secretive.

LIZARDS (pages 52-88) are small to moderately large reptiles with long bodies, long tails and usually with four well-developed legs; a few lizards, however, have small, weak limbs and others are limbless and snake-like in appearance. Lizards have dry, scale-covered skin and their toes are clawed (features which immediately distinguish them from the similar-shaped salamanders). They have closable eye-lids and an external ear opening behind each eye (features which can be used to distinguish limbless lizards from snakes). Many will defend themselves by biting if disturbed.

WORM-LIZARDS (page 89) were at one time considered to be strange lizards, but are now believed to belong neither to lizards nor snakes. They are like large scaly earthworms, with cylindrical, legless bodies that appear to be segmented like worms, and tiny hidden eyes. There is only one species in Europe, found in Iberia where it lives in burrows in loose soils.

SNAKES (pages 90-114) are small to moderately large reptiles with long, more or less cylindrical, scale-covered, legless bodies. It is the front of the body, not the tail which is elongated (the tail is the part of the body behind the anus). Snakes have no closable eye-lids and no external ear openings. They have mouths which can open extremely widely; many will defend themselves by biting if disturbed, and some are more or less dangerous, with poison fangs.

With the exception of two non-venomous snakes (Worm Snake and Sand Boa) European snakes belong to two large families, colubrid snakes (pages 92-108) and vipers (pages 109-114). As most (but not all) colubrid snakes are non-venomous and many vipers are dangerously venomous, it is useful to be able to distinguish between the two families. The scales on the top of the head of a colubrid snake are large, plate-like and always arranged in the same regular pattern; the scales on the top of vipers' heads are more or less fragmented into small scales, irregularly arranged. Unfortunately adders (the most widespread viper species) are intermediate between the two, and have some large scales, but even adders do not have the totally regular, all large scales of the colubrids (see illustration in the glossary on page 12).

 TORTOISES, TERRAPINS & TURTLES (pages 115-121) are small to large reptiles with very distinctive 'shells', made up of a more or less domed section above (the carapace), and a flat piece on the underside (the plastron). The shell is formed of interlocking bony plates which in most species are then covered with horny, shield-like scutes. Head, limbs and tail are all covered with scales.

What's on a page

Once you have decided to which group your reptile or amphibian belongs, turn to the pages where the species of that group are described and illustrated. By comparing the information on relevant pages you can make a positive identification.

On most pages you will find one species described and illustrated. Its common name and scientific (Latin) name are both given at the top of the page, together with its length, from the tip of the head to the tip of the tail. Four boxes provide information about the species, information which makes identification possible. The first box provides details of features or combinations of features characteristic of that animal. The second box provides supplementary information on its biology and habits. The third box provides information on its distribution, and a distribution map is provided for quick reference (either for the whole of Europe or for southern Europe, whichever is relevant); and finally the fourth box describes some of the related species or gives details of species with which this reptile or amphibian might be confused. On some pages related species are also illustrated.

Less common species

Also scattered through the book are pages of less common species, providing information on some of those that are less widely distributed. The Wall and Rock Lizard sections of this kind are particularly large because the Mediterranean region harbours many of these lizards, often with each species found only in one small area or group of islands.

Specimen page

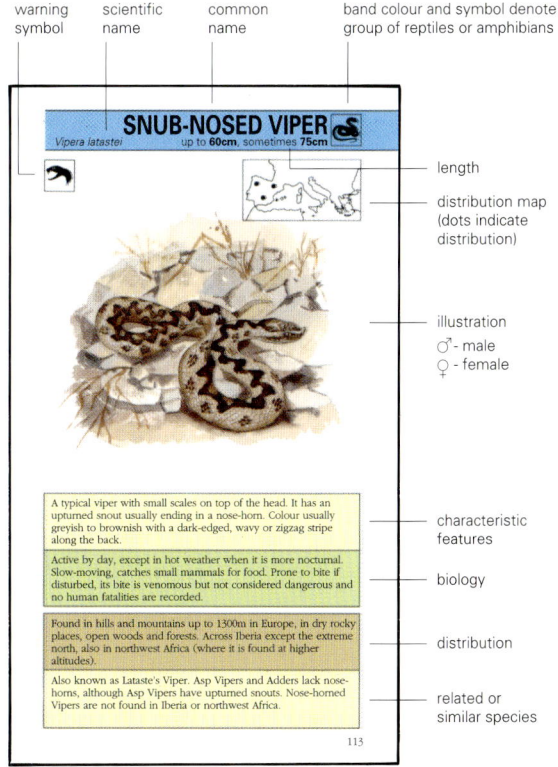

Illustrated glossary

Salamander (male)

soft, moist skin
no claws on toes

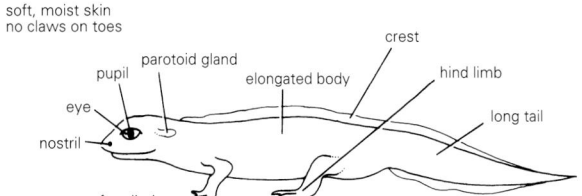

Hind foot of Spadefoot Toad

Frog (male)

soft, moist skin
no claws on toes

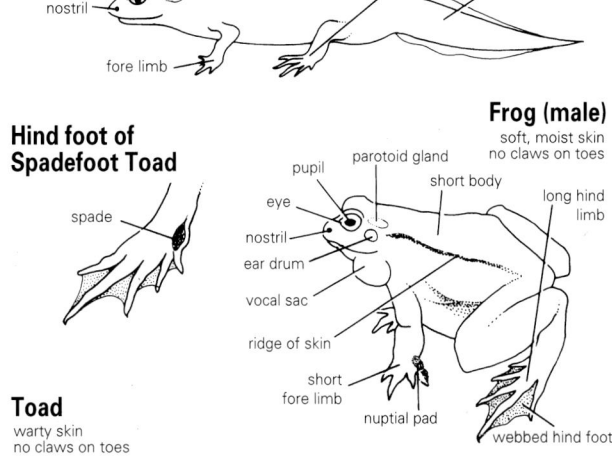

Toad

warty skin
no claws on toes

Snake heads

(from above)

COLUBRIDS
e.g. Grass Snake

VIPERS

Asp Viper   Adder

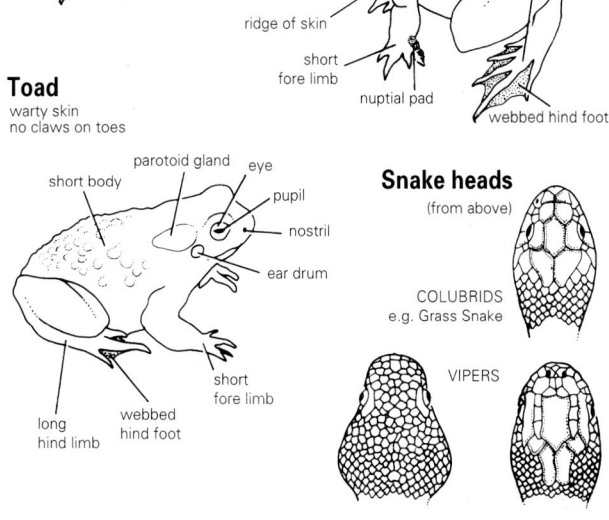

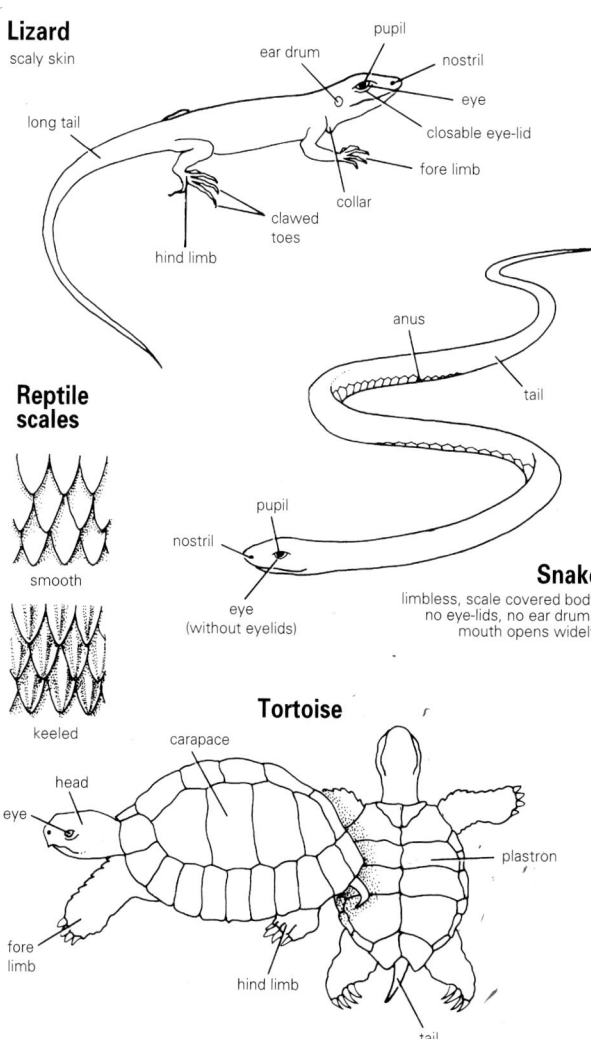

Biology of amphibians

There are about 45 species of amphibians in Europe, in two major groups, salamanders and newts (about 20 species), and frogs and toads (about 25 species). These animals are generally considered to be the most primitive of the terrestrial vertebrates; they are cold-blooded, with soft, scale-less, permeable skin. Most live on land as adults, generally in damp places since their permeable skin is not waterproof, and few can tolerate dry conditions. The majority return to fresh water to breed, the females laying eggs in water; the young develop as tadpoles in the water. Tadpoles breathe with gills at first but soon develop lungs; and all land-living adult amphibians use lungs to breathe. None of them live in the sea.

Cold-blooded

Amphibians are cold-blooded, that means they have to use the environment to maintain their body temperature (unlike birds and mammals which can create their own body heat). They cannot get warm by basking in the sun (as reptiles do) because they would dry out, but where they live, in damp places, the temperature tends to stay relatively constant, as it does in water. Those amphibians that live in northern Europe hibernate in winter, and those in the south often aestivate (remain in a kind of resting state, often in mud) in summer. Many are more active at night, but day-active species tend to be out and about in the morning and evening rather than in the heat of mid-day.

Feeding habits

Most adult amphibians are carnivores, hunting insects, molluscs, worms and other small creatures. Many catch their food with their sticky tongues. Because of their cold-blooded life-style, amphibians do not need as much energy as mammals or birds, therefore do not need to feed as often, and can manage quite nicely while only catching prey intermittently.

Breeding habits

Children all over Europe know that tadpoles appear in ponds in spring. They are young amphibians, hatched from the eggs laid by the females, in a breeding pattern common to many amphibians.

To take frogs as an example, male and female frogs congregate in the same ponds as their ancestors have done, probably since before Man came to Europe. The male clasps the female around the waist, and sheds his sperm over her eggs as she releases them, quickly fertilizing them before the sphere of jelly around each one swells. Once the jelly swells, the eggs are enveloped in the familiar clumps of frog spawn. The tiny embryos develop inside the spawn, until each egg contains a comma-shaped tadpole which emerges about two weeks after the eggs were laid. The tiny tadpoles cling to the remnants of the jelly, feeding on it and on the algae which grows on it, until they develop enough strength to swim away. By this time their gills are covered by gill-covers and not visible, and soon their tails are well developed, they have little round bellies and they swim actively about the pond. The tadpoles feed on algae and pond-plants for a while, then switch to being carnivores, hunting tiny water creatures, feeding on dead fish or frogs, even eating each other in lieu of other prey. Their hind legs develop, followed later by fore legs, then the tail disappears and the tadpoles assume the shape of tiny frogs in a process of change known as metamorphosis.

Many other amphibians follow this pattern with variations; many toad females (accompanied by their male partners) lay their eggs in long strings of spawn instead of in clumps, others singly or in small clusters, but their tadpoles develop in much the same way.

Salamander and newt breeding habits and development are a little different. Male salamanders and newts produce little packets of sperm which they leave on water plants after elaborate courtship displays to their females; the females then pick up the packets and their eggs are fertilised internally. They then lay single eggs on water plants. Their tadpoles are slender (with no rounded bellies), and they have external gills, visible until they metamorphose into the adult shape. Another difference is that salamander and newt tadpoles develop their fore legs first and their hind legs later in their development. And their metamorphosis is a much less dramatic process than in frogs and toads, not surprising because the tadpoles look much more like the adults to start with.

Life cycle of a frog

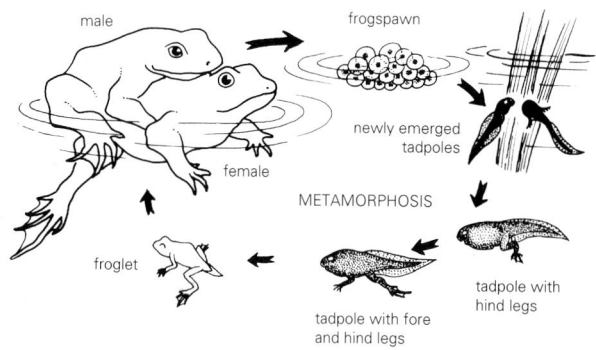

Biology of reptiles

There are about 75 species of reptiles living in Europe, not including the marine turtles which swim in the Atlantic and Mediterranean Seas. They include the tortoises and terrapins (5 species), lizards (about 50 species), worm-lizards (1 species) and snakes (about 27 species). They are generally considered to be more highly evolved as a group than the amphibians, better adapted to life on land and more successful.

They are cold-blooded, but their bodies are covered with a sort of 'coat of mail' of impermeable scales or plates; and they can withstand dry conditions - some species to a greater extent than many other terrestrial animals - living in dry, inhospitable rocky or sandy places.

Their breeding habits are also adapted to life on land; males and females mate so that eggs are fertilized inside the female's body; the eggs are then surrounded by a shell before she lays them, usually in clusters buried in sand, soil, rotting tree trunks etc. The eggs of tortoises, terrapins and geckos are hard-shelled, other reptiles lay soft-shelled eggs. Most reptile females show no more interest in their young once the eggs are laid, but a few will guard their eggs until they hatch. The young develop inside the shelled eggs, in their own little protected environment until they come to resemble miniature adults, when they emerge to take up independent life. A few lizards and snakes do not lay their eggs; instead, the young develop to an independent size inside the female before they are born. This process, known as viviparity, is frequently described in other books as 'bearing live young'. Though that phrasing is not particularly appropriate (after all, an egg is also alive and a young version of the adult, and no animal bears dead young unless something goes wrong).the term is used in this book to save space.

Cold-blooded

Like amphibians, reptiles are dependent on the environment to maintain body temperature, but unlike amphibians they have scaly skin that is impervious to water, and are therefore not susceptible to drying out in the sun. Many raise their body temperature by basking, lying in the sun to absorb heat; they are most likely to be seen basking in the spring after emerging from hibernation, or in the early morning in summer, warming up after the night.

In central and northern Europe, reptiles must hibernate in winter, but southern species may be active throughout the year. However the daily patterns of these southern individuals changes from winter to summer; they may be active during the day in winter, but become more nocturnal in summer or only be out and about mornings and evenings, taking shelter from the heat of the sun at midday, under stones, in crevices etc.

Skin shedding

Reptiles shed the outer layers of their skin regularly, as part of their way of growth. In the north, the first shedding of the year takes place soon after emergence from hibernation. Lizards shed their skin in small fragments, but snakes often shed theirs in one piece, and snake skins may be found in the wild in summer (when they are feeding and growing most actively). Young animals shed their skin more often than adults since they are growing faster. In the week or so before the skin is shed the animal becomes duller, its pattern blurred and its eyes rather opaque, but after shedding the animal is at its brightest with distinct markings and clear eyes.

Feeding habits

Like amphibians, most reptiles are carnivores. Lizards often catch insects, spiders, millipedes, worms and other small creatures. Tortoises and terrapins are more omnivorous, catching insects and other invertebrates, but also eating leaves and fruit. Many snakes hunt lizards, small mammals or nestling birds for their food; their young may take insects.

Venomous snakes use their venom fangs when hunting; the venom is not primarily for defence but for paralysing and killing their prey. Although the fangs of non-venomous snakes contain no venom, they are still effective for stabbing and holding prey animals. Some snakes, traditionally boas, but also others (like Smooth Snake and Four-lined Snake for instance) wrap their prey animals in their folds, constricting their breathing until they die.

VENOMOUS SNAKES may use their venom mostly for hunting, but they will also bite if threatened. They have been given this warning symbol in the illustrations. If you have any doubt about the identity of a snake you encounter, we suggest you do not approach it (many of the non-venomous snakes will also bite hard if threatened and their bites are not pleasant, even if not life-threatening). Any snake bite can produce symptoms of shock, even if no venom has been injected.

Bites from most vipers swell if venom has been injected, and may induce sweating, giddiness and vomiting; they require medical attention as soon as possible. However the venom will spread more rapidly if the bitten person moves about a lot. We suggest that you remain calm, move the affected area as little as possible, and get to a hospital quickly.

Some of the colubrid snakes are also venomous, but they are back-fanged snakes (the venomous fangs are at the back of the mouth, whereas in vipers the fangs are at the front). They cannot bite as effectively as vipers, the poison is not as dangerous as viper venom, but even so, medical attention for a bite would be a good idea. All the poisonous snakes are indicated as such in the text, together with their danger levels.

OLM
usually **20-25cm**

Proteus anguinus

Large aquatic salamander that retains feathery, salmon-pink gills into adult life. Body long and cylindrical, pale in colour; the tiny eyes are covered with skin. Limbs poorly developed, the hind ones with two toes, fore limbs with three.

This salamander lives only in underground streams and lakes, sometimes deep underground, occasionally washed out into the light. Feeds on aquatic crustaceans. Females may lay eggs or give birth to live young.

Found in caves, in the underground water systems of limestone mountains. Occurs only along the northeastern Adriatic coast, from the Istrian region of former Yugoslavia, south to Montenegro; and in one cave in northeastern Italy.

No similar European species.

ITALIAN CAVE SALAMANDER
Hydromantes italicus — up to **12cm**

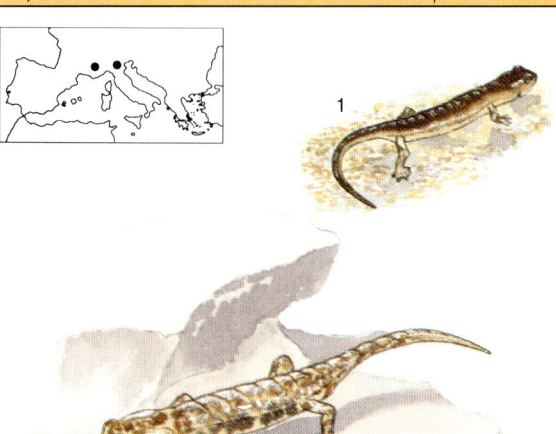

Smallish salamander with smooth skin, wide head and large eyes. The feet are partly webbed, with stubby toes. It has a sticky, extensible tongue with which it catches insects.

Nocturnal, hiding under stones or in crevices by day, climbing over vertical rock faces to hunt by night. Females lay eggs on land and young hatch as miniature adults.

Usually found in cool damp caves, often where water runs over rock surfaces; also in moist shady places under stones or logs. Rocky limestone areas of northern and central Italy, south of the Po Valley, west to Maritime Alps of southeastern France.

Sardinian Cave Salamander *H. genei* (**1**) is similar but grows up to 13cm long; it lives in cool wet caves in the mountains of Sardinia, mainly occurring in the south and east, usually in limestone areas up to 1000m.

FIRE SALAMANDER
up to **20cm** *Salamandra salamandra*

Large, handsome salamander; glossy black, spotted or striped with large, bright yellow or orange blotches. Tail relatively short; toes short and stubby. There are large parotoid glands behind the eyes. Skin moist with irritant secretion.

Nocturnal. Slow-moving, hiding by day under logs or stones, emerging only after rain. Females give birth to live young (tadpoles) in spring, in streams or pools; tadpoles develop in water until they metamorphose.

Found in damp deciduous woods with leaf litter, rarely far from water. In hills and mountains up to 2000m; more common at lower elevations. Across much of central and southern Europe from Denmark to Iberia, Italy and Greece. Absent in British Isles.

A very variable species, with several subspecies, the **spotted form** (**1**) being most widespread. **Banded form** (**2**) is common from northern Spain through southern France to Switzerland. Dark, almost unspotted individuals may resemble **Alpine Salamanders**.

ALPINE SALAMANDER
Salamandra atra — up to **16cm**

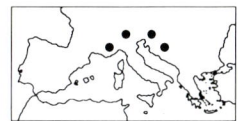

Glossy, uniformly black salamander with large parotoid glands. Its body appears to be segmented.

Nocturnal and secretive, hiding by day in mosses, under stones or logs, often emerging after rain. Slow-moving, hunting slugs, beetles, worms. Females do not lay eggs, but instead give birth to live young which resemble tiny adults (5cm long), on land.

Found in mountains, usually at altitudes between 700-2000m, but also up to 3000m. In moist places, damp deciduous woods but also above the tree-line, in mosses and under stones. In the Alps, and the mountains of Albania and the former Yugoslavia.

May be mistaken for a dark **Fire Salamander** (opposite), but these are usually found at lower altitudes and almost always have at least a few yellow or orange spots.

SPECTACLED SALAMANDER
7-11cm *Salamandrina terdigitata*

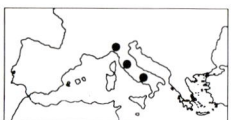

Small salamander with large eyes, a long tail and four toes on each foot. The body appears to be segmented. It has a dark back and throat, pale, dark-blotched belly and a triangular yellow mark on the head. Undersides of legs and tail bright red.

Nocturnal, more often seen in winter than in summer, hunting at dusk. In danger, it may turn on its back to display its bright belly. Females lay clusters of eggs in streams in early spring; emerging tadpoles develop in water till they metamorphose.

Found among damp stones or in dense leaf litter, usually near small streams, in woods with dense undergrowth. On the western slopes of the Apennines in Italy, up to 1300m in altitude, from Liguria to Naples. Most common around Genoa.

All other European salamanders and newts have five toes on the hind feet (four on the fore feet).

SHARP-RIBBED SALAMANDER
Pleurodeles waltl   usually **15-20cm**, up to **30cm**

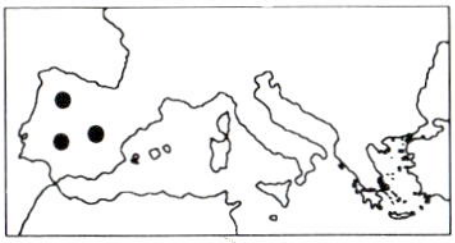

Heavily built salamander, with rough skin and rounded, flattened head. Body is yellow-grey to olive with dark blotches, and has a distinctive row of yellow or orange tubercles along each side, each tubercle above a rib tip.

Mainly nocturnal and aquatic, rarely leaving the water. Slow-moving, feeding on anything that moves. Females lay eggs in clumps in the water at any time of year; tadpoles develop for about four months before metamorphosing.

Found at the bottom of ponds, lakes, ditches and marshes, among dense vegetation, buried in the mud if the water dries up in summer. Widespread in Iberia, except the north and northeastern areas. Also found in Morocco.

This is one of the largest amphibians in Europe. Young individuals may resemble **Pyrenean Brook Salamanders** (p.24), but those are only found in the Pyrenees.

PYRENEAN BROOK SALAMANDER
uusually up to **16cm**　　　　　　　　　　*Euproctus asper*

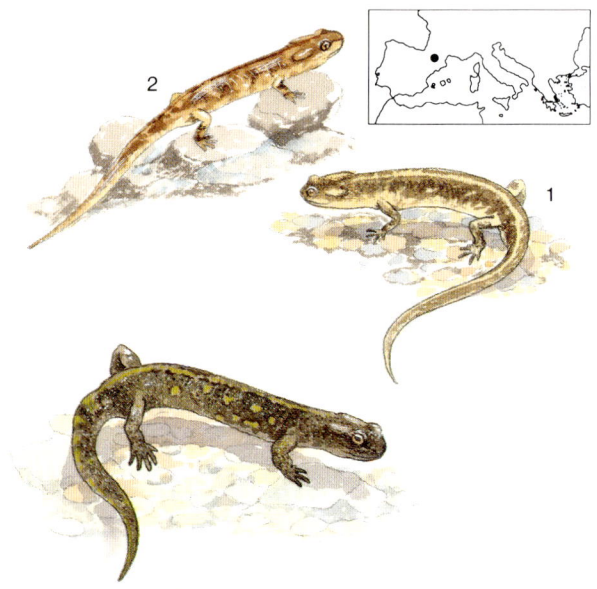

Rough-skinned, quite robust salamander with a long tail. Parotoid glands absent. Muddy brown or greyish in colour, usually with light-coloured or yellowish markings on the back and sides, sometimes with a yellowish stripe on its back.

Mainly active at night, hunting worms and snails; hiding by day under stones or in gulleys. Females lay eggs in clear cold water in spring; tadpoles live in the water for up to a year before they emerge as salamanders.

Found in or beside cold mountain streams or lakes. In Pyrenees, at altitudes of 250m to 3000m, usually between 700 to 2500m, where ice and snow can prevail for seven or eight months of the year. These salamanders cannot tolerate high temperatures.

One of three Brook Salamanders in Europe, all mountain species found in or near running water. Pyrenean is the largest. **Sardinian Brook Salamander** *E. platycephalus* (**1**) grows up to 14cm long, **Corsican Brook Salamander** *E. montanus* (**2**) up to 11cm.

GOLD-STRIPED SALAMANDER
Chioglossa lusitanica — up to **13-15cm**

A very slender, elongated salamander with a long tail and prominent eyes. Brownish in colour with two gold or copper-coloured stripes running along the back, merging into a single stripe on the tail. Belly grey or brown.

Mainly nocturnal, hiding in moss or under stones by day. It has a very long, sticky tongue with which it catches insects. Quick for a salamander, scuttling away like a lizard if disturbed, often into water. A strong swimmer.

Found in isolated colonies, near streams and springs with dense vegetation around. In wooded mountain country, at altitudes up to 1300m, in northwestern Iberia.

No similar species.

GREAT CRESTED OR WARTY NEWT
usually **12-16cm** *Triturus cristatus*

Large, dark newt with coarse skin. Usually dark brown or grey, often sprinkled with white dots, with a yellow or orange belly, and dark spots or blotches all over. Breeding males have high spiky crests on body and tail, and a bluish stripe on the tail.

Found in or near weedy ponds or slow-moving water, hiding under stones or logs by day on land. If handled they produce a foul-smelling secretion. They feed on worms, snails and insects. Females lay eggs in water in spring; tadpoles develop in water.

Found across much of Europe north to central Scandinavia, but absent from southern France, Iberia, Mediterranean Islands and Ireland. Rare in Great Britain. Found in lowlands in the north, but at altitudes of up to 2000m in the south of its range.

A variable species, varying in colour and pattern. Several sub-species occur; Northern Crested Newt (from central Fance northwards and in Great Britain), Alpine Crested Newt (Alps), Danube Crested Newt (Danube basin), Southern Crested Newt (Balkans).

MARBLED NEWT

Triturus marmoratus — up to **14cm**

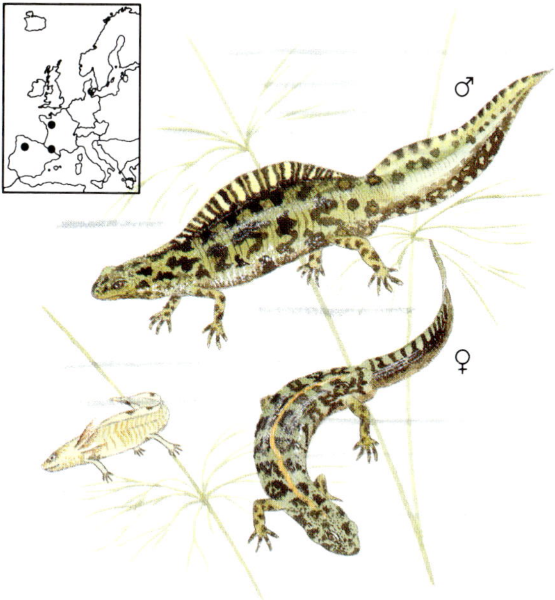

A distinctive newt with a vivid green back, marbled in black. Belly marbled-grey or brown, sometimes pinkish. Terrestrial animals feel dry and velvety, and have an orange stripe along the back. Breeding males have a black-barred dorsal crest.

Nocturnal, hiding by day. They return to small deep, weedy pools or ponds to breed in spring, and may remain in the water into summer. Females lay their eggs singly on water plants (like other newts) and the tadpoles develop in water.

Found for much of the year in woods and heaths. A mainly lowland species, found mostly at altitudes up to 1200m, throughout Iberia and in southern and western France.

Where their ranges overlap, these newts may form hybrids with **Great Crested Newts** (opposite). The characteristics of the hybrid individuals will be intermediate between those of the two parent species.

PALMATE NEWT
up to **9cm**

Triturus helveticus

Small newt with an olive or pale brown back, often with black spots. Belly has a central silvery yellow or orange stripe with a few weak spots. Throat is pinkish, unspotted. Breeding males have a low crest, orange stripes on the tail and heavier spots.

Found in or near ponds and pools, in heathland or woods, also in coastal areas. They enter the water to breed in spring, females laying single eggs from which the tadpoles emerge to develop in the water.

Generally found at higher altitudes than Smooth Newt, up to 1000m in the north of its range, up to 2000m in the south. It occurs in western Europe, from Scotland in Great Britain to northern Iberia, east to northern Germany. Absent from Ireland.

As well as the features mentioned above, breeding Palmate Newt males are unique in having black webs on their hind feet and a black filament on the tail. No other male newts have these features.

SMOOTH NEWT

Triturus vulgaris

7-11cm

Smallish newt with yellow-brown or olive back and lighter belly with a central orange stripe. It has three grooves on top of the head, often dark spots on belly and throat, and a dark line across each eye. Breeding males have a crest and dark spots.

Most common newt over most of its range and one of the most terrestrial, spending much of the year in damp places on land, under stones, in crevices or logs, in woods, gardens, hedges. Females lay eggs in shallow, weedy ponds and ditches in spring.

Usually a lowland species especially in the north of its range, but occurs up to 1000m high in the south. Found across much of Europe, north to central Scandinavia. Absent from Iberia, southern France, southern Italy and the Mediterranean Islands.

Palmate Newt (opposite) and Smooth Newt females are similar, but the latter have orange bellies and spots on the throat, while Palmate Newt females are more delicately coloured with a silvery yellow or orange belly and a pinkish, unspotted throat.

ALPINE NEWT
up to **12cm**

Triturus alpestris

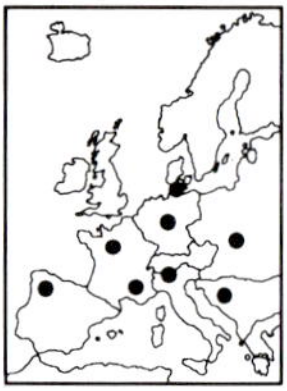

Medium-sized newt with a dark brown or grey back, and uniformly deep yellow to red belly; belly almost always without spots. Flanks often lighter in colour with many dark spots. Breeding males have low, yellow, black-spotted crests and blue flanks.

Usually aquatic; found in or near pools or slow-moving water, usually near the bottom. On land it lives in cool, damp places, emerging in the dusk to hunt, wandering abroad more than many newts. Females lay single eggs in water in spring.

Found across central Europe, from the French coast to eastern Europe, and from central Denmark south to northern Italy and Greece. Also in the mountains of northern Spain. In hills in the north, but mountains in the south, often above 2500m.

Montandon's Newt *T. montandoni* (**1**) is another alpine newt, but one found only in the Carpathians and Tatra mountains. It is smaller, lighter in colour, and its yellow to orange belly often has spots on the sides. It has three grooves on its head.

BOSCA'S NEWT

Triturus boscai

up to **10cm**

Small newt. Male has a lightish yellow-brown back, female a grey-brown back, both marbled with dark spots. In both sexes, the belly has a clear yellow-orange to orange-red stripe, bordered by lighter, black-spotted bands.

Quite active newts, feeding on small water creatures. They breed in spring, the females laying their single eggs in the water, and tadpoles developing there. Breeding males do not develop crests or special colouring.

Found in hilly country or in the lowlands near hills, in or near cool, clear streams or pools. In western and central Iberia.

Palmate Newt (p.28) is more delicately coloured, with a pale silvery yellow or orange belly, and no spots on the throat. **Alpine Newt** (opposite) is larger and has no spots on the belly. Both these overlap with Bosca's Newt in the northwest of its range.

31

ITALIAN NEWT
up to **7.5cm**

Triturus italicus

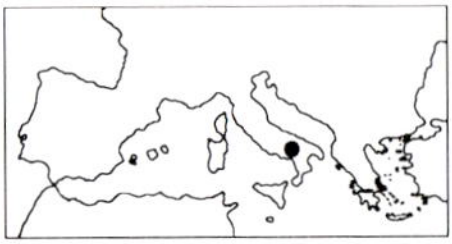

Very small newt. It has a brownish back with lighter flanks, all covered with dark spots; the throat is yellow or orange, the colouring extending onto the sides of the head, towards the eye. Belly similar in colour to, but paler than the throat.

In the breeding season males have a crest on the tail; both sexes develop gold spots on the flanks and a gold spot behind each eye. They breed in still ponds, the tadpoles developing in water. They may become sexually mature while still tadpoles.

Adults leave the water to hide in damp places outside the breeding season. Found in the southern half of Italy, from sea-level to 1500m

The Italian Newt is the smallest European newt. **Smooth Newt** (p.29) is the only other found within its range, and is a larger animal; its belly is darker than its throat and its breeding males have a crest on the back.

PARSLEY FROG

Pelodytes punctatus — up to **5cm**

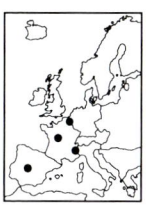

Small warty toad, pale grey or olive with irregular, darker green markings. Often smells of garlic. Eyes have vertical pupils. It has relatively long hind limbs which reach beyond the eyes; and almost webless hind feet.

Nocturnal, emerging after rain. It is agile, can leap well and is a good swimmer. Females lay jelly-bound strings of eggs in water in spring; tadpoles develop in water until they metamorphose.

Terrestrial and found in damp places outside the breeding season, hiding by day under stones or in burrows in damp places, often near water. In Iberia, through France and into western Belgium and northwestern Italy.

Although it looks like a **Common Frog** (p.44), this little toad is related to the **Spadefoots** (p.34/5) - like them, its eyes have vertical pupils. The similar **Midwife Toad** (p.39) is plumper, with relatively shorter hind legs (the heel does not reach beyond the eye).

33

WESTERN SPADEFOOT
up to **10cm** *Pelobates cultripes*

Large, plump toad with smooth skin and a prominent black spade (sharp-edged, flattened tubercle) on each hind foot. Back grey or white to yellow, extensively blotched with green or brown. Eyes silvery or greenish, with slit-like, vertical pupils.

These toads hide in deep, vertical burrows dug in sandy soil. They burrow backwards at high speed, using the spades on their hind feet; the burrow collapses behind them. Females lay eggs in water in spring, in bands of jelly wound around plants.

Nocturnal outside the breeding season. Found in marshy areas near open water in western and southern France, and in Iberia, often near sandy coasts. Sometimes seen on the surface in large numbers after rain.

Common Spadefoot (opposite) is smaller with a pale-coloured spade, a marked lump on the back of its head and has brown, never green, markings. **Eastern Spadefoots** (opposite) are not found in France or Iberia.

COMMON SPADEFOOT

Pelobates fuscus — up to **8cm**, usually smaller

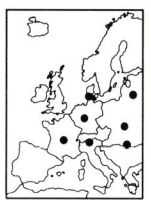

Plump toad with smooth skin, a large pale spade on each hind foot and a large lump on the back of the head. Back may be grey or brown to yellow or whitish, extensively blotched or striped with brown. Eyes golden or coppery with vertical pupils.

Nocturnal outside the breeding season. Most active in wet weather, puffing up, smelling of garlic, standing on hind legs and squealing if threatened. Females lay bands of eggs in water in spring; tadpoles (the largest in Europe) develop in water.

Found in lowland, often cultivated areas, in loose or sandy soil, in burrows like the Western Spadefoot. From northern France across central Europe to Russia, north to Denmark, south to the Alps and northern Balkans. Absent from southern Europe.

Eastern Spadefoot *P. syriacus* (**1**) occurs in the Balkans and Greece; it grows up to 9cm long, has a pale spade but no lump on the head. It varies in colour from yellowish to pale grey or white, with green or brown blotches, sometimes stripes.

35

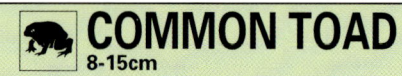 # COMMON TOAD
8-15cm

Bufo bufo

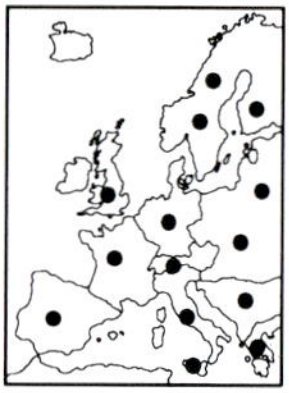

Largest toad in Europe, with warty skin and uniform or blotchy colour. Usually sandy brown to red-brown with a lighter, sometimes marbled belly. Eyes deep yellow or copper with horizontal pupils. Parotoid glands slightly oblique (not parallel).

Hides by day, emerging at dusk to feed on worms, slugs and insects. Males croak. Usually walks, but hops if threatened. Returns to shallow ponds in spring to breed. Male clasps the female while she lays her eggs in strings of toadspawn.

Found on land for much of the year, in a variety of dryish places; individual toads often live in one spot. A common amphibian found across most of Europe and Great Britain. Absent from Ireland and many of the Mediterranean Islands.

Southern Common Toads are often larger than their northern counterparts, with spinier skins. **Natterjack** (opposite) and **Green Toads** (p.38) are generally smaller with distinctive markings, and their parotoid glands are parallel.

NATTERJACK TOAD

Bufo calamita — usually up to **7-8cm**

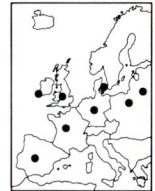

Small, warty toad with short hind legs, brownish or greyish in colour with darker markings, and often a bright yellow stripe on the back. The prominent parotoid glands are roughly parallel to each other. Eyes silver-gold, with horizontal pupils.

This toad runs in short bursts, instead of walking or hopping. Nocturnal, appearing at dusk, males croak in chorus (like a ratchet) at night. Females lay strings of eggs in late spring, in shallow ponds; tadpoles develop quickly.

Found across western Europe from Iberia to Finland and southern tip of Sweden. Scattered in Great Britain and southwestern Ireland. Often in sandy places or near the sea in the north, but in a variety of places in the south, up to 2000m in Iberia.

Common Toad (opposite) is larger, with no yellow stripe, and has oblique parotoid glands. **Green Toad** (p.38) is similar in size but has distinctive green markings.

37

GREEN TOAD
up to **10cm**

Bufo viridis

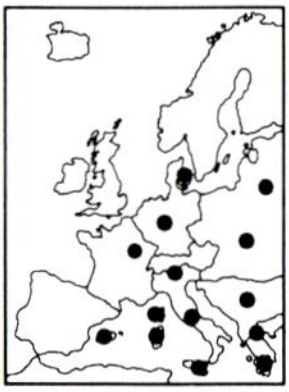

A warty, distinctive toad, pale greyish with extensive green blotches and red tubercles. Eyes have a horizontal pupil. The parotoid glands are parallel. Females are larger and plumper than the smaller, slimmer males.

Mainly nocturnal. Found around dwellings, in orchards, farm land and scrub, or hunting insects round lights at night. Males trill like crickets at night in spring and summer. Females lay strings of eggs in jelly in ponds or slow streams, in spring.

Generally prefers dryish or sandy soils, in lowland areas. Found across eastern Europe, west to Italy and the Balearic Islands in the south, to the southern tip of Sweden, Denmark and eastern France in the north. Very common in the south.

Natterjack (p.37) is similar in size but has shorter legs and a yellow stripe on the back. **Common Toad** (p.36) is larger, duller and slower. **Eastern Spadefoot** (p.35) has similar markings, but has a pale spade on each hind foot and vertical pupils in the eyes.

MIDWIFE TOAD

Alytes obstetricans — up to **5cm**

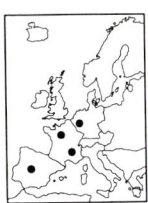

Small, plump toad, varying from grey to olive or brown with small dark, greenish markings. There is a vertical pupil in each eye and three small tubercles on the palm of each hand. Males carry strings of eggs around their hind legs in summer.

Males call to each other at night. They follow females around in spring and summer until one embraces her; she lays her eggs on land and the male carries the eggs until they are ready to hatch; then he takes them to water, where the tadpoles develop.

Found in woods, gardens, dry stone walls and rock piles, hiding by day in crevices, under stones or in burrows. They live in western Europe, from northern France and Germany south to the Alps and throughout Iberia, at altitudes up to 2000m.

Iberian Midwife Toad *A. cisternasii* is similar but has only two tubercles on each palm; it often lives in burrows in sandy places, in central and western Iberia. The **Parsley Frog** (p.33) is not as plump as the Midwife Toads and has relatively longer hind legs.

YELLOW-BELLIED TOAD
3-5cm *Bombina variegata*

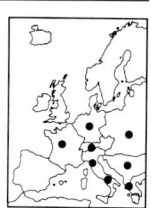

Small, warty, aquatic toad; its distinctive yellow or orange belly has blackish or blue-grey markings. Finger-tips usually bright-coloured also. Back varies from brown or grey to olive or yellowish, the warts often ending in black spiny points.

Mostly active by day, often many found together, males calling to each other in summer. They breed in spring in water, females laying small groups of eggs on water weeds. One may turn on its back and exude a distasteful skin secretion if threatened.

Found in shallow water, at edges of rivers and streams, ponds and ditches, in lowland and hilly areas. Across most of central and southern Europe, from the French coast eastwards. Absent from Iberia, southern Greece and most Mediterranean Islands.

The related **Fire-bellied Toad** (opposite) has a black belly with bright red markings; dark or pale (but not brightly coloured) finger-tips, and its warts are not spiny.

FIRE-BELLIED TOAD
Bombina bombina — 3-5cm

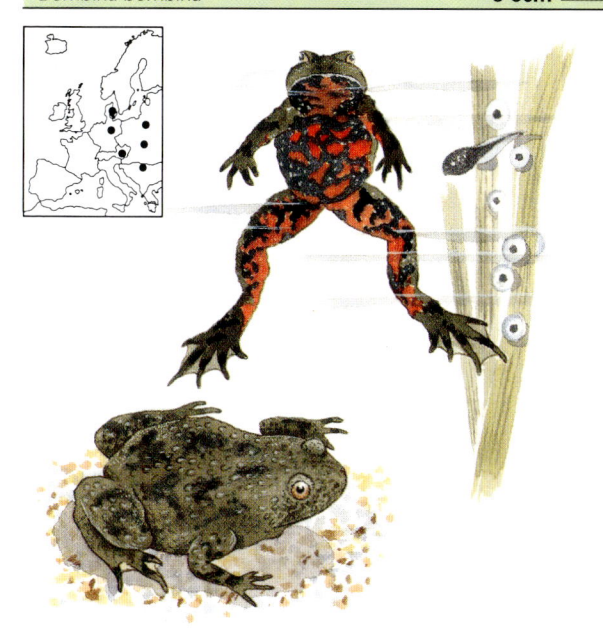

Small, aquatic, warty toad; its belly is black with white spots and bright red or red-orange markings. Finger-tips are not brightly coloured. Warts are not spiny.

Mostly active by day, often found in large numbers, the males calling to each other throughout the summer. Its skin secretes a burning toxin. Females lay eggs on water weeds in summer.

Exclusively a lowland species, found among water plants, in or beside still, shallow water, from small ponds and lakes to swamps and marshes. In Eastern Europe, west to Finland and central Denmark and south to Bulgaria.

Yellow-bellied Toad (opposite) has a yellow or orange-yellow belly, brightly coloured finger-tips, and spiny warts. It is also found at higher altitudes, in more western and southern areas of Europe. The ranges of the two toads overlap in the east.

PAINTED FROG
6-7cm

Discoglossus pictus

A plump, shiny frog, very variable in colour (grey, olive, brownish or yellowish) with darker light-edged spots. Other features include an inconspicuous ear-drum, round or triangular pupils in the eyes, and a disc-shaped tongue.

Active day and night, often seen sitting in water with their heads just above the surface. Males may croak softly. Males embrace females at breeding times; females lay very small eggs several times a year and tadpoles develop quickly.

Found in or near shallow water of pools, rivers and streams, marshes, even in brackish water. Throughout much of Iberia (except the northeast), also in the south of France, Sicily and Malta. And in northwest Africa.

The similar Tyrrhenian Painted Frog is found in the islands of Sardinia, Corsica, Giglio, Montecristo, and the Iles d'Hyeres. Painted Frogs can be distinguished from **Common Frog** by their round pupils, inconspicuous ear-drums and disc-shaped tongue.

IBERIAN FROG

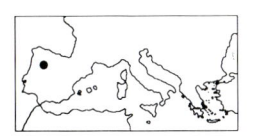

Rana iberica — up to **7cm**

A rather small, often plump frog, similar to the Common Frog but with more widely spaced ridges on its sides. Variable in colour, often grey-brown or red-brown with a dark mask across each eye; it may or may not have other darker markings.

Similar in its way of life to the Agile Frog, and equally agile, leaping away if disturbed. Males croak quietly. Females lay eggs in frogspawn in cold running water in early spring. Tadpoles are very like those of Common Frogs.

Found in mountains, in meadows or forests, often in oak woods, in or near cold running water, streams or springs. In northwestern and central Spain, and in northern Portugal.

Iberian Frog is one of several Brown Frog species living in Europe (others are **Common** (p.44), **Moor** (p.45), **Stream** (p.46) and **Agile** (p.47) **Frogs**). All have a dark mask across the eyes, lack vocal sacs, croak quietly, and are more terrestrial than Green Frogs.

COMMON FROG
6-10cm

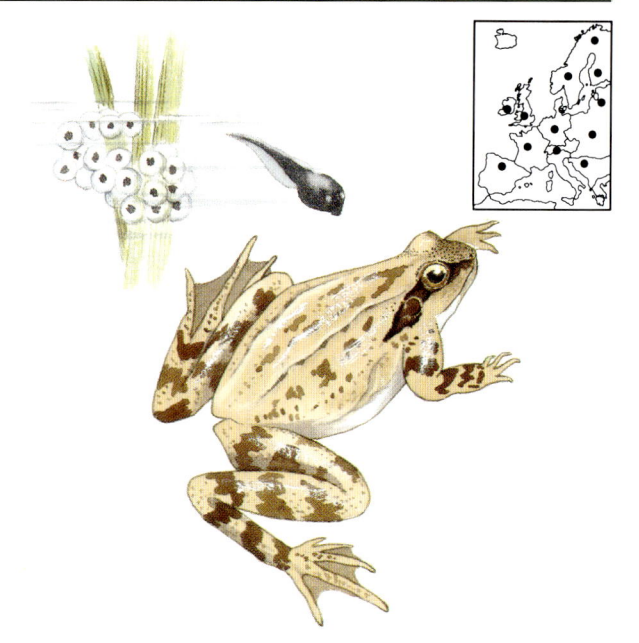

Rana temporaria

Smooth-skinned frog with relatively blunt snout and ridges high on its sides. Grey to brown or olive with darker blotches, dark band across each eye, often with a dark ∧ marking between the shoulders. Eyes have horizontal pupils. Hind legs relatively short.

Active by night; mostly terrestrial, moving on land by leaping; powerful swimmers in water. They return to water to breed in spring, when the males croak softly. Male clasps the female while she lays her eggs in masses of frogspawn.

Lives in many moist places, woods, gardens, marshes; also in water, ponds, canals and ditches. Common and widespread across much of Europe, south to northern Italy and northern Iberia. Absent from southern Balkans, Greece and Mediterranean Islands.

Moor Frog (opposite) is similar but has a more pointed snout, its markings often form stripes, and there is a large, horny tubercle on each hind foot (Common Frogs have a small, soft tubercle).

MOOR FROG

Rana arvalis

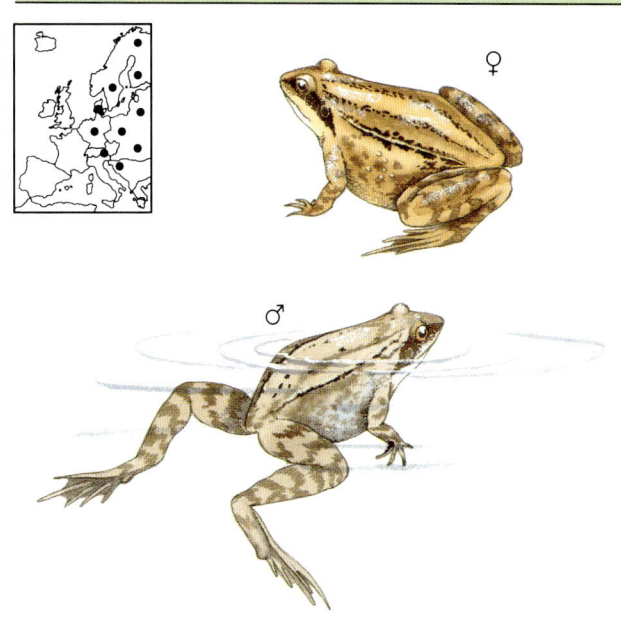

up to **8cm**

♀

♂

Smooth-skinned frog with ridges on its sides and a dark mask across each eye. Snout pointed, hind legs short; a large, hard tubercle on each hind foot. Colour varies, back often has broad stripes or dark markings. Eyes have horizontal pupils.

Agile, leaping on land, swimming in water. Found in bogs and marshes, damp meadows, pools and ponds. They hibernate in winter, returning to water to breed in spring. Males croak quietly, clasping females as they lay masses eggs in spawn.

Found in wetter places than Common Frog, becoming rarer in Europe with the draining of wetlands. Northern France to Sweden and Finland (but not the Norwegian side of Scandinavia), south and east to the Alps, northern Romania and former Yugoslavia.

Common Frogs (opposite) live in drier places; they are less striped in appearance, with a blunter snout and a soft, small tubercle on each hind foot. Their hind limbs are longer.

STREAM FROG
up to **7.5cm**

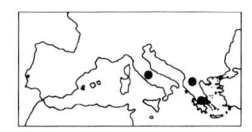

Rana graeca

Frog with relatively long legs, rounded snout, horizontal pupils, and dark mask. Often greyish with pale blotches, dark 'Λ' marking across the shoulders and yellow-flushed hind legs. Throat dark with pale central stripe. Ear-drum small and indistinct.

Hides under stream banks, in vegetation etc. Emerges from hibernation in early spring, found in the water for a short breeding season. Females lay eggs in quieter stretches of running water or in small woodland pools.

Most often found in forested mountain areas, on the banks or in cool running water, streams, springs, wet caves. Italy, and the central and southern half of the Balkans.

Similar in appearance to **Common Frog** (p.44) and **Agile Frog** (opposite). They are distinguished from each other by a variety of features, including size and position of ear drum, length of legs, colour of throat, spacing of nostrils and spacing of shoulder ridges.

AGILE FROG
Rana dalmatina

up to **9cm**

Quite slender frog with very long hind limbs, pointed snout and horizontal pupils. Large ear-drum lies close behind each eye. Colour often pinkish or yellowish, sometimes with a few dark spots. There are dark bands across eyes and legs. Throat pale.

Found in damp, often shady places, wet meadows, woodland edges near water, reed beds. Active at dusk and at night. Very agile. Breeding groups congregate in ponds in late winter and early spring; males clasp the females as they lay their spawn.

Found across central and southern Europe, from the Atlantic coast of France to the Balkans and mainland Greece. Absent from most of Iberia, most Mediterranean Islands (except Sicily), the British Isles and most of northern Europe.

Italian Agile Frog *R. latastei* (**1**) has a dark throat with a light narrow stripe down the centre; often has pink-flushed limbs and belly, and its small ear drum is well separated from the eye. Found in wet lowland woods in northern Italy and southern Switzerland.

MARSH FROG
up to **15cm**

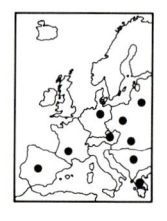

Rana ridibunda

Largest European frog, variable in colour, often green or olive with dark markings, sometimes rather warty. Snout pointed. Eyes close together with no dark mask. Hind foot has small, soft tubercle. Male has a grey vocal sac at each corner of mouth.

Aquatic, gregarious, active night and day, sun-loving, resting on the banks, on lily pads or with heads just out of water. Males noisy, singing in chorus in spring and summer. Females lay eggs in spring, in small masses of spawn under water.

Found in all kinds of ponds and lakes, rivers and streams, ditches. From Germany north to Russia and south to Greece, also in southern France and Iberia. Introduced to Kent and Somerset in Great Britain and Imperia province in Italy.

Marsh Frog, **Edible Frog** and **Pool Frog** (opposite) are all Green Frogs (aquatic and noisy, with vocal sacs, no dark eye-mask). Edible and Pool Frogs are smaller than Marsh Frogs, brighter in colour, with larger, harder tubercles.

EDIBLE FROG
Rana esculenta — up to **12cm**

Smaller than a Marsh Frog, often brighter green or brown, often with a light stripe along the back and dark markings. Thighs marbled in brown or black and yellow. Vocal sacs whitish. There is a hard, often sharp-edged tubercle on each hind foot.

Aquatic, gregarious, active by day and sun-loving like Marsh Frogs. Males sing in noisy choruses in spring and summer. Usually hibernate on land. Females lay masses of eggs in spring, tangled in weed under water.

Found generally in smaller bodies of water than Marsh Frogs, including ponds and marshes. Across central Europe. Absent from most of Scandinavia, Iberia, most of Balkans and Greece and most of the British Isles. Introduced to East Anglia and Kent.

Pool Frog *R. lessonae* (**1**) is very similar, with a similar distribution; it can be difficult to identify frogs as Pool or Edible Frogs with certainty. Pool Frogs are generally smaller (up to 9cm long), with shorter hind legs and larger tubercles on the hind feet.

COMMON TREE FROG
up to **5cm**
Hyla arborea

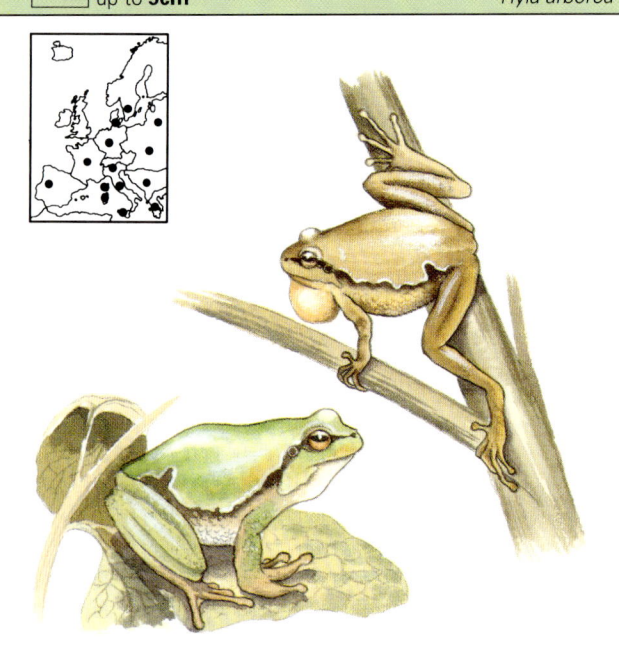

Small climbing frog with smooth skin and long limbs. Fingers and toes have adhesive, disc-like pads on their tips. Usually bright green, with dark stripes from the nostrils along the flanks to the groin and on the limbs; throat and belly whitish.

Usually active at night. Tree Frogs live in bushes, trees or reeds, often far from water. Males sing noisily, especially in summer, expanding their large vocal sacs. They return to water in spring to breed, females laying eggs in rounded clusters.

Found across Europe and Asia, throughout Italy, the Balkans, Greece and the Greek Islands, Sardinia, Corsica, Sicily. Absent from the north and the British Isles, from parts of southern and eastern Spain, southern France and the Balearic Islands.

Stripeless Tree Frog (opposite) replaces the Common Tree Frog in northern Africa, southern Iberia, southern France and the Balearic Islands. It is very similar in appearance, but has dark stripes only across the eyes and ear drums, not down the flank.

STRIPELESS TREE FROG

Hyla meridionalis — up to **5cm**

A small, climbing, smooth-skinned frog with adhesive pads on its toes and usually bright green in colour, very similar to the Common Tree Frog. But it has no dark stripe on its flanks, only across the eyes and ear drums.

Lives a similar life-style to Common Tree Frog, but found at lower altitudes where the two occur together (although their ranges are more complementary than overlapping). Both species can change colour, from green to yellow or brown.

A southern species, living in southern Iberia and southern France, the Balearic Islands and northwestern Italy. Also in northwest Africa, Madeira and the Canary Islands.

Common Tree Frog (opposite) has a stripe along each flank and thigh, as well as across eyes and ear drums. It has a much wider distribution, found much farther north and east in Europe, and in Asia.

MEDITERRANEAN CHAMELEON
up to **20-30cm**   *Chamaeleo chamaeleon*

Distinctive, unmistakeable lizard. Slow-moving, with a flattened, leaf-shaped body; clasping, pincer-like hands and feet; and prehensile tail. Bulging eyes swivel independently. Rapidly changes colour to match its background and mood.

Climbs about slowly in bushes, but hard to see; if disturbed it becomes dark and inflated, with its mouth open. Catches insects with its extensible, sticky tongue. Females descend to the ground in late summer to lay eggs which they cover with soil.

Found in dry scrubby places in southern Iberia and Crete.

No similar species. Many other chameleons are found in Africa.

SLING-TAILED AGAMA

Agama stellio — up to **30cm**

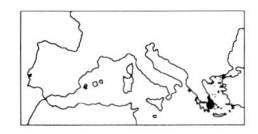

Large, spiny lizard with a short, flattened body and triangular head. The spines on body and tail occur on transverse rows of tubercles. Colour may be grey to brown, often with diamond-shaped yellow blotches along the back and a barred tail.

Sun-loving lizard that climbs and basks in the sun on dry-stone walls, trees and rocks, in dry places like olive groves and rocky hillsides; characteristically it bobs its head every so often. It will run into hiding if disturbed.

Often common where it occurs, in Greece and the Greek Islands (around Thessaloniki, on some of the Cyclades and on Corfu). It is more widely distributed in Egypt, Syria and Asia Minor.

Agamas are a common group of lizards in Asia and Africa, but this is the only one found in Europe.

MOORISH GECKO
up to **15cm**

Tarentola mauritanica

Plump, robust lizard with flattened head and body, and broad adhesive pads along the toes (broadest at the tips). There are rows of tubercles over body and tail, making it look spiny. Usually light brown or grey with dark bands on body and tail.

Agile climber, in and around houses, on dry-stone walls, wood piles, cliffs and trees. Active by day in winter, more by night in summer; attracted to insects around lights. Males fight in spring; females lay eggs in rock clefts or under tree-bark.

Found in the Mediterranean region, in warm dry lowland areas especially around the coast, from Iberia to the Ionian Islands and Crete, also the coast of North Africa. In Iberia it is also found inland.

Turkish Gecko (opposite) is paler and slimmer, with toe-pads that do not extend to the tips of the toes, and the toes end in obvious claws. The smaller, secretive **Leaf-toed Gecko** (p.56) lives only in Sardinia and Corsica and a few localities nearby.

Swindon Libraries
01793 707120
Thank you for using
North Library

Borrowed Items 18/10/2018 16:53
XXXXX81006

Item Title	Due Date
*Frogs	09/11/2018
*practical guide to setting up your marine tropical aquarium	09/11/2018
*Reptiles amphibians : a practical guide to over 180 of he most familiar, B	09/11/2018
*Setting up a tropical aquarium week by week	09/11/2018
*Reptiles and amphibians	09/11/2018
Art matters	28/10/2018
Brain book	04/11/2018
Crisis in the Cotswolds	04/11/2018
Social psychology for dummies	05/11/2018
field guide to the reptiles and amphibians of Britian and Europe	06/11/2018

* indicates items borrowed today
Thankyou for using this unit

TURKISH GECKO

Hemidactylus turcicus

up to **12cm**

Slimmer than **Moorish Gecko** (opposite), with toe-pads that do not extend to the tips of the toes. Toes end in obvious claws. Also paler, rather translucent, with darker blotches on the back and a banded tail. It has rows of whitish tubercles on back and tail.

Mostly active at dusk and at night, often in and around houses. May be attracted to the insects around lights at night. A fast and agile climber. Females lay their eggs in rock crevices or beneath the bark of trees.

Found on dry-stone walls, buildings, cliffs and rocks, on trees, palms and agaves, around the coasts of Mediterranean Europe, from southern Iberia to the Middle East, all around the islands and North Africa.

Paler than any of the other geckos in the Mediterranean, with obvious claws on the toes as well as toe-pads.

EUROPEAN LEAF-TOED GECKO
up to **6-8cm** *Phyllodactylus europaeus*

The smallest European gecko, slim-line in shape, with a long, flattened body and no tubercles on the soft, granular skin. Toes have adhesive pads only at their tips. Often brownish or grey, and marbled in yellow; or it may be yellowish all over.

Nocturnal and secretive, most active at dusk, intolerant of strong sunshine. Found in olive groves and scrub, usually hiding under bark of dead trees or logs, under stones or in dry-stone walls.

Found on Corsica, Sardinia and neighbouring smaller islands, and on the nearby Italian mainland. Also occurs on islands off the coast of Tunisia.

The other European geckos are larger, more obvious. They have tubercles on back and tail. **Moorish Gecko** (p.54) has toe pads which extend all along the toes; and the toe pads of the **Turkish Gecko** (p.55) do not extend to the tips of the toes.

KOTSCHY'S GECKO

Cyrtodactylus kotschyi — up to **10cm**

Typically gecko-like in shape, but without the adhesive pads on the toes. Instead it has characteristic kinks in the toes. Usually grey or brown with dark v-shaped bands, and rows of tubercles, on back and tail.

Active by day in winter, especially morning and evening; more often at night in summer. More often found on the ground than other geckos, but also climbs on dry-stone walls, cliffs and buildings. Not often found inside houses.

Most often found in dry rocky or stony places, in southeastern Italy, eastern and southern areas of the Balkans, and the Greek Islands.

There are not really any similar species. Other geckos have toe-pads. The somewhat similar **Wall Lizards** (pp.74-81) lack the kinked toes.

ALGERIAN SAND-RACER
20-30cm *Psammodromus algirus*

A fairly small lizard with a long, rather stiff tail. Back and flanks have large overlapping scales that are pointed and keeled; there is no collar. Colouring includes metallic brown back, pale belly, and two pale stripes along each flank.

Very agile and fast, active lizard, usually hunting by day around the base of plants or basking in the sun. Well camouflaged. Males have one or two bright blue spots on each shoulder, and red throat and cheeks in the breeding season.

Found in dense bushy vegetation, dense oak and pine woods, among gorse and heather, across Iberia (except on the north coast) and in a small part of southern France. Also in northwest Africa. It squeaks and may bite if handled.

Spanish Sand Racer (opposite) is much smaller. Other related lizards lack the large, overlapping scales.

SPANISH SAND-RACER
Psammodromus hispanicus　　　　　　　　**10-12cm**

Small lizard, with large, overlapping, keeled scales. Collar weak, obvious only on the sides. Colour metallic brown to grey or ochre, either uniform or with a broken pattern of white stripes and blackish bars running along the body. Belly pale.

A ground-living lizard found in open areas broken by patches of low growing vegetation, also in sandy and gravelly places. It runs fast across such areas, hides among plants if threatened and squeaks if handled.

Found across Iberia except the north, in the lower Rhone Valley in France and on the French Mediterranean Coast.

Algerian Sand Racer (opposite) is much larger with different colouring. **Wall Lizards** (pp.74-81) do not have large overlapping scales but they do have a distinct collar.

DESERT RACER
up to **15cm**

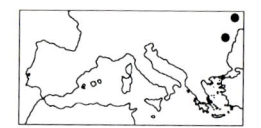

Eremias arguta

Medium-sized, quite stout lizard, grey or grey-brown in colour, with a broken pattern of stripes or rows of light, dark-bordered patches on its back. Tail is short (for a lizard), and thick at the base. Belly white.

Hides from the heat of the day in summer, in burrows or under stones, beneath tall grasses in the steppes. Also hibernates in these retreats in winter. Hunts spiders and insects for food, like many other smallish lizards.

Found in open sandy country, steppes, on sandy river banks, dunes and coasts in the Danube Delta and on the Black Sea coastline in Romania. Also across southern Russia to the Ural and Caucasus Mountains.

No similar species live in Europe.

SPINY-FOOTED LIZARD
Acanthodactylus erythrurus   **18-20cm**

Medium-sized lizard, variable in colour. Adults grey or brown, with up to 10 pale longitudinal streaks separated by dark blotches. The **young (1)** are black with pale stripes, red thighs and a red tail, well camouflaged in desert conditions.

Found hiding around plants, in burrows or beneath stones in the heat of summer; basking in the sun in spring or autumn. Runs long distances if disturbed. Its toes have fine fringes of spiny scales which prevent the feet from sinking into sand.

A very alert, ground-living lizard of open sandy or rocky places, bare of plants or with sparse vegetation. Found across Iberia except in the north, also in northwest Africa.

One of about 20 *Acanthodactylus* species found in north Africa and the Middle East; this is the only one to occur in Europe. Some of the others have much more obvious fringes on their feet.

DALMATIAN ALGYROIDES OR KEELED LIZARD
up to **21cm** *Algyroides nigropunctatus*

A small, dark lizard, like a wall lizard but with large, rough, keeled scales on its back; flank scales are smaller. Usually dark grey-brown to red-brown above, with black spots. Adult male has blue throat and eyes, orange-red belly.

Active by day but secretive, preferring shady places in summer, hiding if disturbed. It climbs on rocks and dry stone walls, shrubs and trees, often in scrub, olive groves, vine-yards, fields and ruins, sometimes in inhabited towns and villages.

Found all along the eastern coastline of the Adriatic Sea, from the Ionian Islands in the south to Corfu, through northwest Greece to Albania and north to Istria in the former Yugoslavia.

One of four Algyroides lizards in southern Europe. They may be mistaken for **Wall Lizards** (pp.74-81), but Algyroides are darker and more uniform in colour, and they all have the large keeled back scales.

OTHER ALGYROIDES
Algyroides species

Spanish Algyroides
A. marchi (**1**) Up to 15cm long. Small lizard, its large back scales only weakly keeled. Coffee-brown, often with a dark line on the back; males may have a yellow belly. Secretive, living in mature pine forests around fast-flowing streams. In southeastern Spain.

Pygmy Algyroides
A. fitzingeri (**2**) 10-12cm long. Very small, dark, rather flattened lizard, with large (for its size), keeled & pointed scales on back & flanks. Found in scrub & on rocky slopes, often hiding under bark, around the bases of oaks or olives. Corsica & Sardinia.

Greek Algyroides
A. moreoticus (**3**) Up to 15cm long. Small lizard with large, pointed, keeled scales on back & flanks. Both sexes dark-brown or red-brown with a lighter belly; male has dark, white-spotted flanks, female more uniform in colour. Active by day but secretive, preferring shade, hiding in walls, leaf litter among bushes, often on north slopes or near water. Ithaca & Zante, Peloponnese, Cephalonia.

SNAKE-EYED LIZARD
14-16cm *Ophisops elegans*

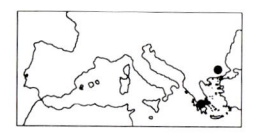

Small lizard with no closable eye-lids (the large eyes will not close when touched). It has no collar on the throat. It varies in colour, but often has two pale stripes on each flank, the upper one bordered with black blotches.

Active by day. A ground-living lizard, found on arid hillsides and fields with sparse vegetation or scrub, sometimes in vineyards. It dodges from one clump of grass to another if threatened, but is generally not fast-moving.

Found in the southern Balkans, Turkey and the extreme northeastern area of Greece (including Thasos). Also in the Middle East and around the eastern Mediterranean to Libya.

The related **Wall Lizards** (pp.74-81) and **Algyroides** (pp.62/3) have a collar, a transverse fold of skin on the throat; they can close their eyes (like most lizards). Several other species of snake-eyed lizards live on the steppes of western Asia and in northeast Africa.

SAND LIZARD
Lacerta agilis
18-24cm

Stocky lizard with a short deep head, and a line of narrow scales running down the back. Colour variable, usually with a grey or brownish back, a band of spots on the back and more on the flanks. Males often have green flanks, females brown.

A mainly ground-living lizard, often inconspicuous, hiding in burrows. Active morning and late afternoon. Found in dry places usually in or near low dense vegetation; hedgerows, roadsides, pastures, overgrown coastal dunes, gardens; also in heather.

Found across most of Europe north to central Scandinavia, but rare in Brittany and southern France and in Great Britain where it is mostly restricted to the southern heaths. Absent from Italy, the southern Balkans and most of Iberia.

A form with a red-brown back occurs in Europe but not in Britain. **Green Lizard** (p.68) is larger, more green overall and not just green on the flanks. **Viviparous Lizard** (p.71) is smaller, less stocky, grey or brown with different patterns.

OCELLATED LIZARD
40-80cm *Lacerta lepida*

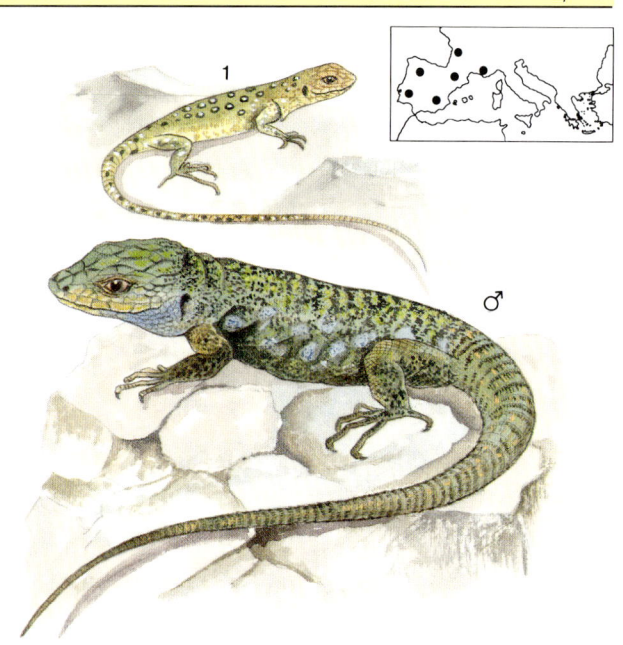

A large lizard, adults recognizable by size alone. Usually green, sometimes grey or brownish, with reticulated black markings on body and bright blue blotches on each flank; throat usually greenish. Males have a broad, massive head.

Active by day. Found in dry rocky scrub, old olive groves and vineyards, open woods and thickets. Mostly on the ground but also climbing on dry-stone walls and rocks; hiding in crevices or rabbit burrows if threatened. Very agile and fast.

Found across Iberia and in southern France, also the extreme northwestern tip of Italy. Northwest Africa. At altitudes up to 1000m in the Alps and Pyrenees; up to 2000m in southern Spain and Africa. More common in lowlands than in highlands.

Young (1) are green with black-bordered, white spots all over the body. Smaller Ocellated Lizards, **Green Lizards** (p.68) and **Schreiber's Green Lizards** (opposite), and their young, can be similar, but can often be distinguished by their colour patterns.

SCHREIBER'S GREEN LIZARD
Lacerta schreiberi   about **20-30cm**

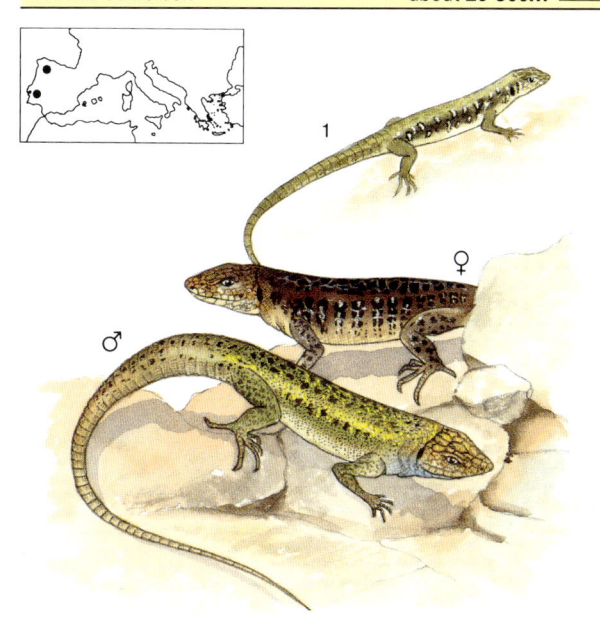

Large lizard. Males green with black spots on back, smaller ones on flanks; throat often blue (also blue in some females). Females usually brownish; their back and sides have dark blotches, the blotches often arranged in three rows.

Like other green lizards, these animals are agile and fast-moving, active by day, climbing with confidence on rocks and among bushes; they feed on snakes and smaller lizards, as well as insects and fruit. Males fight during the mating season.

Found in overgrown bushy places, on hillsides, roadsides, banks and walls, among brambles, in damper, more overgrown places than Ocellated Lizards where the two occur together. In northern and western Iberia.

Young (1) are green with black-edged white or yellow spots on the flanks; tail often yellow or orange. Adults may resemble smaller **Ocellated Lizards** (opposite), but these often have blue spots on the flanks; and females are usually green, without blotches.

67

GREEN LIZARD
30-40cm

Lacerta viridis

Large lizard. Males usually green with a blue throat and black speckles on the back. Females vary in colour, northern ones mostly uniform brown or green, southern ones often with two to four light stripes; some have a blue throat.

Found in scrubby places, hedgerows and woods, banks, thickets, vineyards and pastures, hunting and climbing in bushes, basking in the sun. They often take refuge in a tree if threatened, but will bite if cornered. Males fight in the mating season.

Much of Europe from Channel Islands to southern Russia in the north; south to northern Iberia, through Italy, the Balkans and mainland Greece. Also on Sicily, Elba, Corfu, Samothrace, Euboa and Thasos. Often in damp places or in highlands in the south.

Young (1) are brownish, some with light spots, or two to four light lines on the flanks. **Balkan Green Lizard** (opposite) is similar and the two species can be difficult to tell apart in the Balkans, on the eastern Adriatic coastline and on the Greek Islands.

BALKAN GREEN LIZARD
Lacerta trilineata — up to **50cm**

A large lizard. Adults are usually bright green with black speckles on the back. Immature adults and young may be brownish, often with three or five light stripes.

Active, agile and fast-moving. A good climber. Mainly a lowland lizard, found in bushy places, on cultivated land, on dry-stone walls and ruins, and among overgrown sand-dunes on the coasts.

Found in the southern and eastern Balkans, in the Greek Islands and along the Adriatic coastline to Istria in the north.

The similar **Green Lizard** (opposite) tends to live in damper places and at higher altitudes where it overlaps with the Balkan Green. Look for two to four light stripes on females and young (Green Lizards) or three to five stripes on immatures (Balkan Greens).

69

ROCK AND WALL LIZARDS
Lacerta and *Podarcis* species

The largest group of lizards in Europe (about 24 species). All small, usually brown or green, variably patterned in stripes & spots. Difficult to tell apart, because of the way in which they vary, even within a single species. Many live among rocks, in stony places, on dry-stone walls, some climbing on rock faces.

Rock Lizards belong to the genus *Lacerta*, **Wall Lizards** to *Podarcis*. The differences are mostly internal. Species are often most easily identifiable by distribution, as many are restricted to quite small areas.

For instance, the **Maltese Wall Lizard** (**1**) (*P. filfolensis*) occurs only on Malta, Gozo & nearby islets. It lives on dry rocky slopes, roadsides, dry-stone walls & in gardens. A small lizard (16-24cm long) & variable in colour & pattern.

Greek Rock Lizard (**2**) (*L. graeca*) lives only in the Peloponnese, mostly in mountains, often near water, on rocks, screes, road cuttings. A good climber. Up to about 25cm long, it is grey-brown with dark spots, light-spotted dark flanks, & a yellow or orange belly.

VIVIPAROUS OR COMMON LIZARD
Lacerta vivipara **15-18cm**

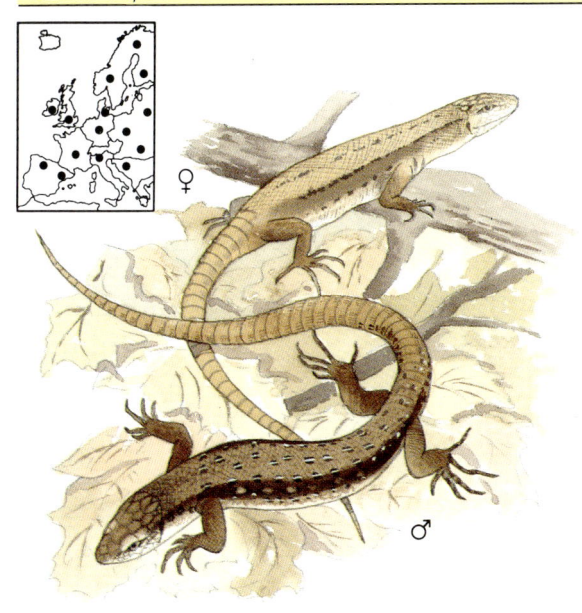

Small lizard with short legs, long body, small rounded head and serrated collar. Back scales large and keeled. Usually grey or brown; often males have dark-edged light spots, females broken stripes. Males and some females have dark spots on the belly.

A ground-living lizard seen in woods and pastures, fields, grassy dunes, hedges, banks and sea-cliffs in the north, often more restricted to damp places in mountains in the south. Females give birth to live young in summer.

Likes cool, damp places but basks in the sun to maintain body temperature. Widespread and common across northern and central Europe from Ireland and arctic Scandinavia to Asia, south to northern Iberia, northern Italy and northern Balkans.

The commonest of the rock lizards, the only rock or wall lizard in the north. Also widespread, **Common Wall Lizards** (p.74) are more flattened, with a longer snout and smooth-edged collar; their females resemble those of Viviparous Lizards but lay eggs.

OTHER ROCK LIZARDS
Lacerta species

Iberian Rock Lizard
L. monticola (**1**) 18-19cm long. Similar to **Common Wall Lizard** (p.74) but more robust. Iberian Rock Lizards vary in colour, but many individuals have a distinctive green belly. Young have a blue tail. Found in the mountains of north, west & central Iberia, above 1100m, often near or above the tree-line; they are able to withstand the long cold winters & cool wet summers of the area. Good climbers in damp places, around rocky hillsides & streams, in juniper scrub, among heathers & pines.

Bedriaga's Rock Lizard
L. bedriagae (**2**) 15-20cm long. Flattened lizard with unkeeled back scales (**Italian Wall Lizard** (p.76), also found on Sardinia, has keeled scales on the rear back). Greenish, brownish to grey with black markings; young often have a bright blue-green tail. Occurs from 600 to over 2000m on rocky hills, screes, cliffs, dry-stone walls & streamside boulders, in Corsica & Sardinia.

OTHER ROCK LIZARDS
Lacerta species

Horvath's Rock Lizard

L. horvathi (**1**) Up to 16-20cm long. Small flattened lizard with pale brown back & throat, & dark sides. Found in damp mountain areas, on rocks, cliffs, limestone pavements, in woods or above the treeline. Northwest mountains of former Yugoslavia & adjoining parts of Italy. Often occurs with **Common Wall Lizard** (p.74).

Sharp-snouted Rock Lizard

L. oxycephala (**2**) Up to 20cm long. Small flattened lizard. Back usually light, dappled brownish, belly blue, tail banded in brown & turquoise. In highland areas & some islands they are much darker. Good climber on sunny cliffs, walls, rock-piles, often around towns & villages. Southwestern area of former Yugoslavia, from sea-level to 1500m, some off-shore islands.

Mosor Rock Lizard

L. mosorensis (**3**) Up to 22cm long. Small flattened lizard. Back usually brownish or olive with darker spots (sometimes all dark), belly usually deep yellow, unspotted. Found in damp rocky places, on north-facing slopes, open woods, and around springs, from 600-1500m, in southwest area of former Yugoslavia.

COMMON WALL LIZARD
15-23cm
Podarcis muralis

Small flattened lizard with a smooth-edged collar, long snout and slightly keeled scales. Colour usually grey or brownish; males have complex patterns of spots with or without stripes; females often have dark flanks and dark stripes.

A rock-climbing lizard often seen on vertical rock faces, dry walls, buildings, ruins and garden walls, in towns, open woods and scrub, also on roadsides and slopes in the south, especially in the mountains. Very agile and alert.

Found across central and southern Europe, from the Channel Islands and northern France to the Balkans, south to central Spain, much of Italy and the Greek Islands. Absent from the British Isles and much of northern Europe.

Several other wall lizards resemble this one, and they are all very variable so can be difficult to identify. They include **Iberian Wall Lizard** (opposite), **Italian Wall Lizard** (p.76) and **Dalmatian Wall Lizard** (p.80).

IBERIAN WALL LIZARD

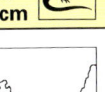

Podarcis hispanica

14-18cm

Small, flattened lizard, usually brown or grey, with whitish to pink or red belly. Throat usually pale with small spots. Many animals are striped, often with one or more dark stripes on each flank; males tend to have spots over the stripes.

Active by day, sun-loving, seen climbing on rock faces and cliffs, walls and parapets. Fast-moving, runs into crevices if disturbed, but bites, defecates or sheds its tail if captured (like other lizards).

Found in Iberia and the western Mediterranean area of France. This is the only wall lizard or rock lizard found in southern Iberia except around Almeria (where the Italian Wall Lizard occurs).

Iberian and **Common Wall Lizards** (opposite) may be difficult to tell apart. **Bocage's Wall Lizard** (p.79) is also similar but Bocage's is less flattened, often with a yellow to salmon belly; it climbs less and lives only in the northwestern corner of Iberia.

ITALIAN WALL LIZARD
20-30cm
Podarcis sicula

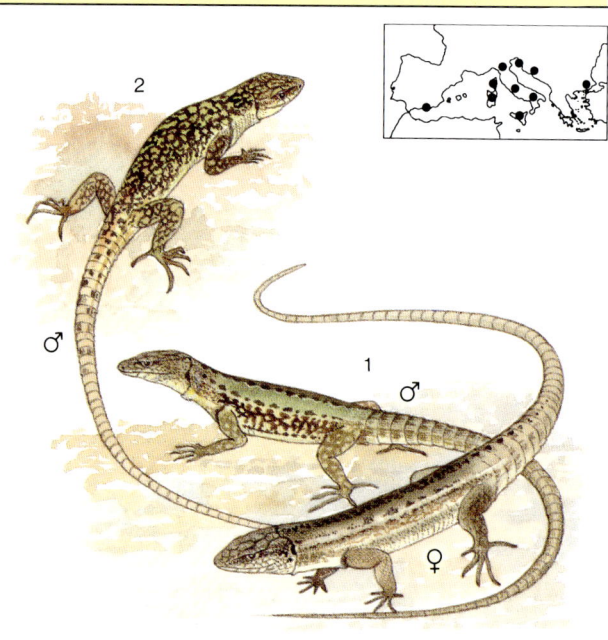

Medium-sized wall lizard, very variable in colour, usually green, yellowish or light brown on the back. Underside usually pale, whitish, without spots (most other wall lizards in the area have spots on the underside).

Active, ground-dwelling lizard, not as shy as many but running into bushes or walls if threatened. Found on roadsides, in vineyards, near the sea or human habitation, where colonies of them may be seen basking in the sun.

Found mostly in lowlands, in grassy and sandy places, throughout Italy, Corsica, Sardinia, Sicily, on the east coast of the Adriatic and on other islands in this area. Also around Almeira in Spain, on Minorca and in Turkey.

In most of Italy and Corsica these lizards are usually streaked in some way (**1**); but in southern Italy, Sicily and Sardinia they are often reticulated (**2**). **Sicilian Wall Lizard** (p.81) is closely related.

BALKAN WALL LIZARD
Podarcis taurica   **14-20cm**

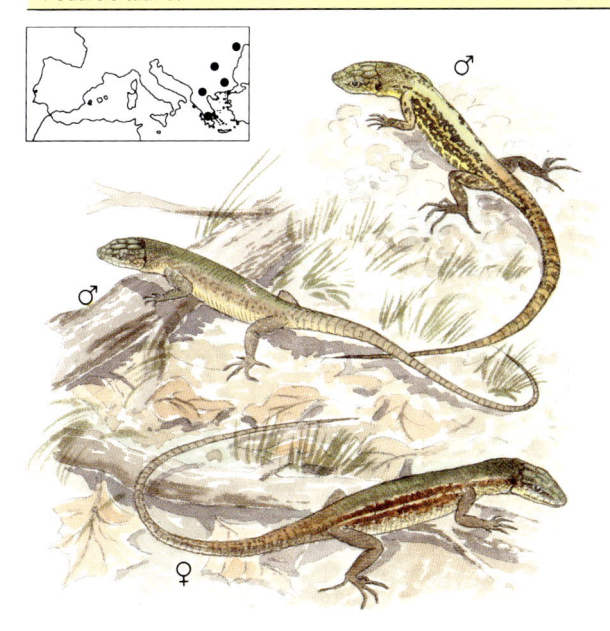

Rather like a small Green Lizard, with a green back, light stripes and a dark-spotted pattern on the flanks. The belly is often whitish and unspotted, but bright red or orange in breeding males. The collar is serrated.

A ground-living lizard, found in dry grassy, often open places but where there is vegetation. Seen basking on roadsides, field edges, or less conspicuously hunting among brambles or crops. Hides in holes or under bushes if threatened.

A lowland species, found across the southern and eastern Balkans Peninsula, from the Greek Islands of the Aegean to the Crimea, but not in the former Yugoslavia.

Dalmatian Wall Lizard (p.80) - which overlaps with Balkan Wall Lizard in northern Albania - is similar but generally smaller with a smoother collar. **Green Lizard** and **Balkan Green Lizard** (pp.68/9) are much larger.

ERHARD'S WALL LIZARD
15-22 cm *Podarcis erhardii*

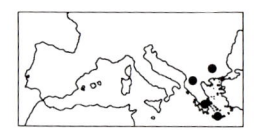

Small lizard with smooth collar, usually brown or greyish with light and dark stripes, especially on the sides. Belly white or yellow, sometimes with dark spots on the throat. Males often have reticulated sides and bright bellies in breeding season.

A mainly ground-living lizard which climbs to some extent, usually found in dry stony places on the mainland, with brambles and other low-growing plants. In the islands it also occurs in open places, dunes and in dense Mastic Tree growth.

The mainland form, described here, is found in the southern Balkans, north to Albania and southern Bulgaria, and south to the Peloponnese. Island forms, found in many of the Aegean Islands, are much more variable in colour, pattern and size.

Erhard's Wall Lizard is the only wall lizard species in the Cyclades and northern Sporades. **Milos Wall Lizard** (p.81) replaces it in the Milos group of islands; the males of this species are dark with distinctive green, blue or yellowish spots.

OTHER WALL LIZARDS
Podarcis species

Bocage's Wall Lizard
P. bocagei (**1**) Similar to Iberian Wall Lizard but more robust & less flattened. Male often spotted, with green back & yellow or orange belly. Females browner & plainer, with stripes rather than spots. Found in the far northwest tip of Spain & northern Portugal, where it scrambles & climbs on rocks, road banks, screes etc.

Lilford's Wall Lizard
P. lilfordi (**2**) Up to 20cm long. Small tough lizard with fine small scales. Mostly brownish or greenish, often with a pattern of dark & light streaks & blotches on the orange flanks. Almost black individuals are also common; they usually have blue bellies. Balearic Islands, mainly on small rocky islets.

Ibiza Wall Lizard
P. pityusensis (**3**) Up to 20cm long. Small, robust, tough lizard, similar to Lilford's Wall Lizard, but with relatively coarse, slightly keeled scales. Usually has a green back with light & dark streaks & spots on the flanks. Ibiza & Formentera, in gardens, fields, ruins & scrub; also on nearby rocky islets. This species has been introduced to Minorca.

OTHER WALL LIZARDS
Podarcis species

Tyrrhenian Wall Lizard
P. tiliguerta (**1**) 16-20cm long. Small, unflattened lizard. Very variable, often striped and/or with spots on back & flanks. Females often brown, males often green on back or sides. Found from sea-level to 1800m on Corsica, Sardinia & neighbouring islands. In dry stony places, roadsides & field edges, scrub & open woods. Partly replaced by **Italian Wall Lizard** (p.76) in damp, lower altitude places.

Dalmatian Wall Lizard
P. melisellensis (**2**) 16-20cm long. Very variable lizard; males usually have a green back & rows of spots on sides & back; females may be green or brown, usually without spots but often with stripes. Climbs a little but mostly ground-living, in dry places, on roadside banks, uncultivated ground, pastures, open woods & scrub. East coast of Adriatic from Italian border to northern Albania, & on many offshore islands.

OTHER WALL LIZARDS
Podarcis species

Sicilian Wall Lizard
P. wagleriana (**1**) 16-25cm long. Usually green backed (females sometimes brown) with pale stripes high on the sides & often with rows of dark spots on the back. Flanks often dappled (especially in males) & males have a red or orange belly. A ground-living lizard found in grassy inland places in Sicily.

Peloponnese Wall Lizard
P. peloponnesiaca (**2**) Up to 25cm long. Rather large for a wall lizard, male with blue blotches on flanks & gold belly, female with gold stripes on shoulders. Lives in dry rocky places, scrubby hillsides, olive groves, on ruins, walls & cliffs. In the Peloponnese.

Milos Wall Lizard
P. milensis (**3**) 16-18cm long. Male has a brown back & distinctive green, blue or whitish spots on flanks, head & throat. Female lighter, with stripes on back & blotches on throat. Found on dry-stone walls, stone piles, often near cultivated ground, also on stony hillsides, in the Milos group of Greek Islands.

OCELLATED SKINK
up to **30cm**

Chalcides ocellatus

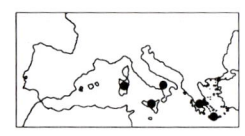

A relatively large skink, with large, glossy scales, long body, thick neck and small, pointed head. Its limbs are short, each with five toes. Buff-coloured or grey with pale, dark-bordered spots or streaks often joined together into cross-bars.

Very quick and agile. Most active morning and evening, warming themselves on stones or hunting for insects, but staying close to cover. They hide under stones or in burrows by day, running if disturbed. Females give birth to live young.

Found in sandy lowland places, often near the sea, behind dunes or beaches. Also in sandy fields, vineyards, scrubland. Sicily, Sardinia, Pantellaria, Malta, Attica and Peloponnese, Euboa and Crete. Near Naples in southern Italy. Northwest Africa.

Greek and Cretan individuals are often smaller (up to 20cm long). Individuals from the western region of the range often have a pale stripe on each shoulder and dark flanks. **Bedriaga's Skink** (opposite) is similar but smaller, and it lives only in Iberia.

BEDRIAGA'S SKINK

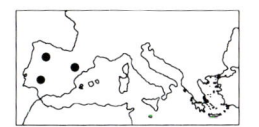

Chalcides bedriagai — up to **16cm**

A long-bodied skink with a small head and large, glossy scales; the short limbs each have five toes. Light brownish or grey with scattered, black-edged light spots. Often there is a pale stripe high on each side.

Secretive, often burrowing into loose sand, hiding in vegetation or under rotting logs. It may be seen basking on stones to gain body heat. Females give birth to live young.

Found most often in sandy, lowland places, often with a good covering of plants where it can hide, but also in country with sparser plant growth, on hillsides, grassy pastures. Across most of Iberia except the north.

Ocellated Skink (opposite) is the only similar species but it is larger and not found in Iberia.

SNAKE-EYED SKINK
9-12cm *Ablepharus kitaibelii*

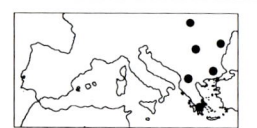

A very small, slender, glossy lizard with short legs and head. Its distinctive feature is its eyes, which have no closable eyelids and so do not close when touched. Brown to olive in colour with darker flanks, and often with small dark markings.

Found in relatively dry places, meadows, woodland clearings especially in oak woods, usually where it can hide or hunt spiders and insects in vegetation or fallen leaves. May be seen basking but timid and quickly retreats into cover if disturbed.

Found in the southern and eastern regions of the Balkans, south to some of the Aegean Islands and east to Asia Minor. It also occurs further north in eastern Europe, to Hungary and Czechoslovakia.

No similar European species. The only other skink found in this area is the **Ocellated Skink**, (p.82) which is much larger with closable eyelids.

THREE-TOED SKINK
Chalcides chalcides

up to **40cm**

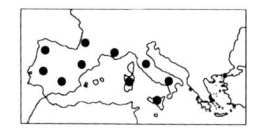

An elongated, snake-like skink, its limbs tiny with three toes each. It has large, glossy scales and a small head; tail ends in a horny tip. Brown, olive or grey, some uniform in colour, others with a varying number of dark and/or light stripes.

Active by day, quick and agile, gliding rapidly through vegetation like a snake and darting into cover if alarmed. But basking in the sun if undisturbed. They hunt molluscs, insects and worms for food. Females give birth to live young.

Found in dry grassy places, grassy roadsides, in vineyards and garigue. Also in damper meadows or near water, especially when near the coast. In Iberia, southern France, Italy, Sardinia, Sicily and Elba. Also in northwest Africa.

No really similar species in Europe; no other European lizard has such tiny limbs. **Snakes** and **Slow-worm** (p.87) lack limbs altogether and Slow-worms move much more slowly.

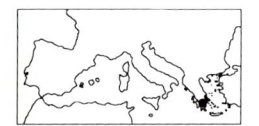

GREEK LEGLESS SKINK
up to **20cm**　　　　　　　　　　*Ophiomorus punctatissimus*

A legless lizard, resembling a Slow-worm, but with shiny scales and a pointed snout. Usually cream or beige above, paler on flanks and belly; with fine dark stripes or rows of dots, most obvious on the tail, less well defined on the back.

A secretive, burrowing lizard. Moves its conspicuous, striped tail if disturbed, attracting any predator to this part of its body, then escapes by shedding the tail and rapidly burrowing its way to safety. Feeds on insects.

Burrows into loose, loamy soil, usually in grassy places with scattered stones. Often more obvious in spring, when it comes to the surface, than in summer when it remains underground or under stones. Found in southern Greece and on Kythera.

Slow-worm (opposite) is larger, differently coloured and patterned, with a blunt snout. **Worm Snake** (p.90) is more slender (like a shiny worm), has tiny eyes on the top of its head, and the tip of its tail is thicker than its head.

SLOW-WORM
Anguis fragilis — 30-50cm

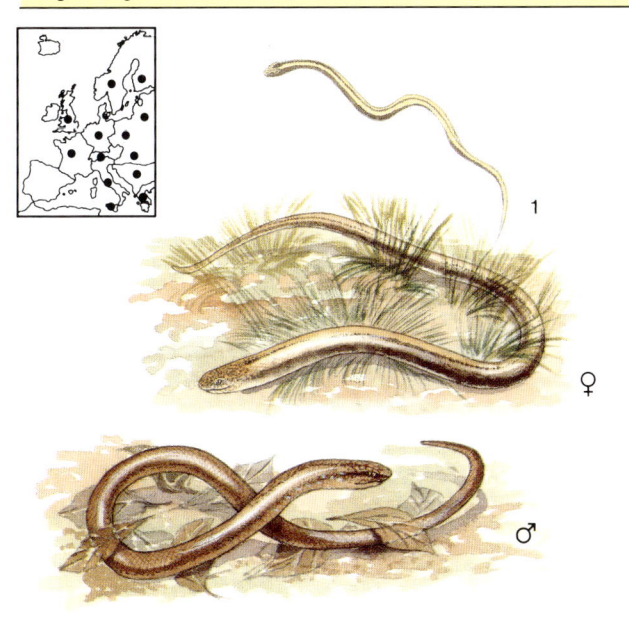

A lizard with a long, legless body like a snake. Unlike a snake it has closable eyelids and its tail breaks off easily. It has very smooth, polished scales and a brown body. Males sometimes have blue spots, females sometimes a dark line along the back.

Secretive, slow-moving, most often seen in early morning or evening or after rain, hunting worms and slugs. At other times it hides in places with good ground cover, under rotting tree trunks, in hedgebanks and thickets, in garden compost heaps.

Common in old woodland, grassy meadows and heaths, also in gardens. Across most of Europe from Great Britain eastwards, north to southern Scandinavia and Finland. Absent from southern Iberia, Ireland, Balearic Islands, Sardinia, Corsica and Crete.

Young (**1**) are distinctive, with a gold or silver back, dark sides and belly, and a dark back stripe. **European Glass Lizard** (p.88) is much larger, faster-moving and has a groove on each flank. **Snakes** lack closable eyelids and their tails do not break off.

EUROPEAN GLASS LIZARD
up to **120cm** *Ophisaurus apodus*

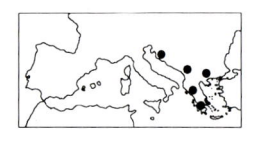

Resembles a giant Slow-worm, with a large, heavy, brownish body, large head and almost no legs (just the tiny remnants of hind legs on each side of the anus). It has closable eyelids (unlike a snake) and a prominent groove on each flank.

Active in twilight and after rain, and can move quite quickly, silently if it is hunting. May also be seen basking in the sun. Its tail breaks off easily but does not regenerate to any large extent.

Found in relatively dry places with some plant cover, open woods, banks and rocky hillsides, dry-stone walls, vineyards and olive groves. In the Balkans, north to Istria in the former Yugoslavia in the west, and east into Asia.

Young (1) are distinctive, grey with dark bars. No other reptiles look quite like this. Slow-worm (p.87) is much smaller and slower. **Snakes** have no closable eyelids and their tails do not break off.

EUROPEAN WORM LIZARD
Blanus cinereus — 15-30cm

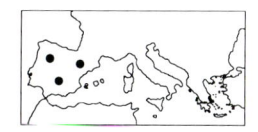

Rather like a dry, scale-covered earthworm in appearance, with an elongated, legless body that appears to be segmented. It has a small head and tiny eyes (hidden under transparent scales). Usually grey or brownish, often tinged with pink or mauve.

Lives in burrows which it digs itself in moist soils. Seldom seen on the surface and only discovered by turning over large stones or logs to uncover a burrow (when it retreats anyway) or when fields are ploughed. Feeds on worms, ants, other insects.

Found in moist, loose, loamy soils in cultivated ground, pine woods. Throughout the Iberian peninsula except the north; also in Algeria and Morocco.

No other similar species in Europe. Belongs to a group of reptiles known as amphisbaenians, that are neither snakes nor lizards but are related to both.

WORM SNAKE
usually up to **30cm**

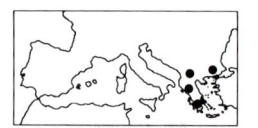

Typhlops vermicularis

Slender, cylindrical snake with a small inconspicuous head and eyes like black dots. Resembles a dry shiny worm more than a snake. Tail short, thickened and ending in a spine. Colour pinkish or yellowish, slightly darker on the back than belly.

A burrowing snake, living mainly underground like a worm, emerging sometimes at twilight or after rain, most often in spring. Feeds on ants, ant larvae, termites and other small underground creatures; the mouth is small. Non-venomous.

Found in open places with loose soil, grass and loose stones, like steppes and meadows; also near the sea. Southern Balkans and mainland Greece, also Corfu, Skyros, Rhodes, Cyprus, some of the Cyclades. Also in the Middle East and northern Africa.

No similar species. Sometimes mistaken for a **Greek Legless Skink** (p.86) which is found in southern Greece, but the skink is much thicker, with a larger head and a distinctive pattern of stripes.

SAND BOA

Eryx jaculus turcicus

up to **80cm**

A stout snake with small, rather glossy scales, a blunt tail and indistinct head. Eyes small with vertical pupils. Usually grey or brown with irregular darker bands on the back. Often a dark Λ on the head and a dark line from mouth to eye.

Spends much of its time in rodent burrows or lying buried in loose soil or sand, perhaps emerging at dusk. Relatively slow-moving if uncovered by day, but faster when it hunts rodents, lizards etc. Females give birth to live young in late summer.

Found in arable land, sandy places, beaches, in places where the soil is loose and the snake can burrow. Southern Balkans and Greece, on some of the Cyclades. North to former Yugoslavia and Corfu in the west, east to southwest Asia. North Africa.

The only boa found in Europe. Like its more exotic and mostly larger relatives (other boas, pythons and anacondas) from other parts of the world, this snake constricts its prey and is not venomous.

HORSESHOE WHIP SNAKE
up to **100-150cm** *Coluber hippocrepis*

Relatively slender snake with smooth scales. Eyes have round pupils and a distinctive row of small scales beneath. Body has a pattern of black oval or diamond blotches in paler areas; often a horseshoe-shaped mark on the neck. Belly yellow to red.

Fast-moving, agile, difficult to approach and apt to bite if caught but not venomous. Active by day, usually ground-dwelling but can also climb in trees or buildings where it may hunt mice. Feeds on small mammals, birds, lizards.

Found in dry rocky places, scrubby hillsides, also in and around buildings. In the southern, western and eastern areas of Iberia, in the island of Pantellaria and rarely in southern Sardinia. Also in northwest Africa.

Some individuals can appear to be almost black. No similar species. The related **Algerian Whip Snake** *C. algirus* (**1**) occurs in Malta in Europe (although its main range is in northwest Africa).

WESTERN WHIP SNAKE

Coluber viridiflavus up to **150cm**, sometimes **200cm**

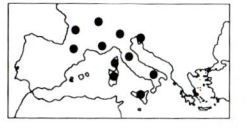

Quite a slender snake with a long tail, smooth scales and round pupils. Black or dark green, more or less speckled with yellow-green, becoming striped towards the tail. Belly yellowish. It can be all black, especially in the south and northeast.

Active by day. Alert, fast-moving, more or less ground-living although it also climbs fast and well in bushes or among rocks. Aggressive and will bite hard if caught. Non-venomous. Catches small mammals, birds, lizards and snakes for food.

Found on sunny rocky slopes, old stone walls and ruins with cover from bushes, in scrub and macchia. In Italy, Sardinia, Corsica, Sicily and Malta. Also northeast Spain, southern half of France, through Switzerland to Istria; rarer in the north.

Young (1) are pale grey or olive with distinctive head markings (bold light lines over a dark background) and often with dark blotches towards the head. **Young Balkan Whip Snakes** (p.95) are very similar to them, although their adult pattern is different.

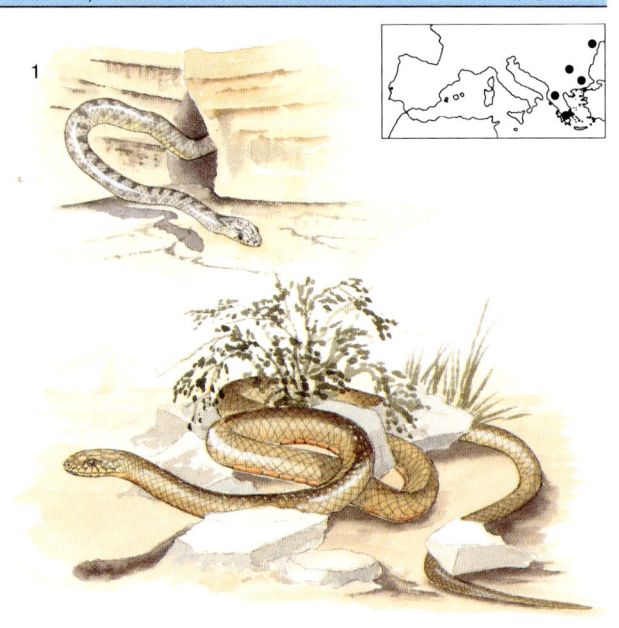

LARGE WHIP SNAKE
up to **200cm**, sometimes **300cm** *Coluber jugularis*

One of the longest European snakes. Colour varies from yellow-brown to almost black on the back, belly yellow to orange. The smooth back scales have light edges or centres, giving the effect of light stripes or a lattice. Eyes have round pupils.

Active by day, most often found on the ground, moving swiftly. Tends to retreat rather than attack but will bite if caught, and not let go. Non-venomous. Catches small mammals for food. Young take lizards and insects.

Found in dry, open rocky places, often with some vegetation, on hillsides, dry-stone walls, in vineyards, gardens and open steppes. Throughout southern Balkans and Greece, many of the Aegean Islands. North to Hungary and the Ukraine, east to Asia.

Young (1) are grey or brown, with a pattern of dark bars on the back and no light stripes on the head; in pattern they are different to the young of **Balkan Whip Snakes**. Adult Balkan Whip Snakes are smaller than adult Large Whip Snakes, and spotted.

BALKAN WHIP SNAKE

Coluber gemonensis — usually less than **100cm**

Rather slender snake with smooth scales and round pupils in the eyes. Colour grey to yellow-brown with dark spots on the fore part of the body; the spots are often divided by light streaks. Tail often has light and dark stripes.

Active by day, fast-moving, gliding along on the ground but also sometimes climbing in bushes. Aggressive and will bite hard if handled. Non-venomous. Feeds on lizards mainly, but will also take small mammals and birds.

Found on shrubby hillsides, overgrown ruins and walls, open woods and vineyards. Along the eastern Adriatic coast from Istria southwards (including many offshore islands and Corfu) to the Peloponnese in Greece. Also Crete, Kythera and Euboia.

Young are very similar to those of **Western Whip Snake** (p.93), with light markings on the head. **Large Whip Snake** (opposite) is larger with a different pattern; its young have dark bars on the back and no light markings on the head.

DAHL'S WHIP SNAKE
up to **100-130cm** — *Coluber najadum*

Very slender snake with a long tail. Grey-green to pale brown in colour on the back with a pale belly. It has a distinctive row of dark spots along each side of the neck; the anterior spots are larger and usually have light rings around them.

Active by day, hiding in crevices at night. A good climber, moving very fast through bushes, also on the ground, hunting small mammals, lizards and insects. Streaks away if threatened, not aggressive or venomous, but may bite if handled.

Found in dry stony places with bushes or tall grasses, open woods and scrub, near overgrown walls. Southern Balkans, Greece and the islands close to the mainland, north along the eastern Adriatic coast to Istria in former Yugoslavia. East into Asia.

No similar species. Other **whip snakes** are less slender and none have the distinctive neck spots.

MONTPELLIER SNAKE
Malpolon monspessulanus — up to **200cm**

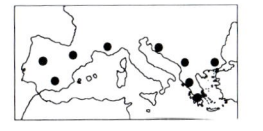

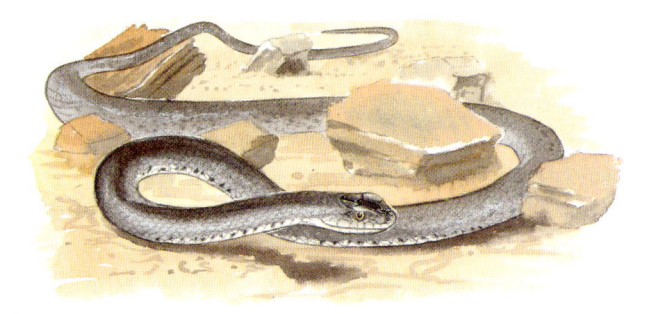

1

A large, more or less uniformly coloured snake, grey or olive to brown or darker. Head distinctive, with a ridge overhanging each eye, and a depression on top of the head between the ridges. It has venomous fangs at the back of the mouth.

Alert, agile, aggressive. Hunts rodents, lizards and other snakes for food. Hisses long and loud if threatened and will strike, injecting venom from its back fangs. Dangerous if handled. Venom causes pain and swelling for a few hours.

Found in dry stony or rocky places where bushes or other plants provide cover, in open woods, scrub, stabilized coastal dunes, overgrown arable land and walls. Iberia, Mediterranean France, Balkans, Greece, many Greek Islands. North Africa. Middle East.

No other snakes have the 'eyebrows' or the depressed head. **Young (1)** often have a pattern of indistinct dark blotches, which can be retained into adulthood in the eastern population; western youngsters tend to lose the blotches as they grow.

AESCULAPIAN SNAKE
up to **150-200cm**
Elaphe longissima

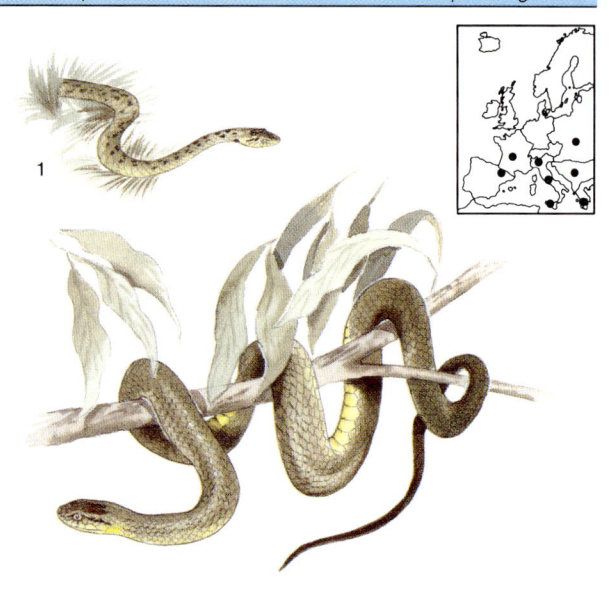

A long, quite slender snake with round pupils. Scales smooth. Usually olive-brown to grey, becoming darker towards the tail. Belly pale yellowish. Scales often edged in white. There may be a dark streak behind each eye, followed by a yellow blotch.

Not very fast-moving but a good climber and swimmer. Active by day and warmth-loving, often found on south-facing slopes in the north. It hunts small mammals, sometimes birds. It may hold its ground if disturbed, and bite if handled. Non-venomous.

Found in dry sunny places, clearings in open woods, among rocks or on old walls. Across central Europe from central France eastwards. Also south to northeast Spain in Iberia, through Italy and Sicily, the Balkans and Greece to the Peloponnese.

Young (**1**) have dark spots on the body and bold dark markings over yellow on the head. Adult **Four-lined Snakes** (p.100) (in the east) and **Ladder Snakes** (in France) are related but both have dark lines on the body and their young are different in pattern.

LADDER SNAKE

Elaphe scalaris

up to **120-150cm**

A large, thickset snake with a short tail, smooth scales and round pupils in the eyes; the snout overhangs the mouth. Adults are more or less uniformly yellow-grey to brown with two dark stripes on the back.

Active by day. Mostly ground-living, also climbs in bushes and rocks. Hides at night and in bad weather, often in a burrow or hollow tree. Quick and agile, usually hunts small mammals, killing by constriction. Bites if handled but non-venomous.

Found in sunny stony, often south-facing places, vineyards and old orchards, dry open woods and scrub, fieldsides, dry-stone walls and rocks. Across Iberia, along the Mediterranean coast of France, in Minorca and the Isles d'Hyeres.

Young (1) are distinctly marked with a dark ladder pattern which fades with age. **Aesculapian Snake** (opposite) is more slender, without lines on the back and has a more rounded snout; its young are spotted.

FOUR-LINED SNAKE
up to **150cm**, sometimes **200cm** — *Elaphe quatuorlineata*

One of the largest European snakes, moderate in build, with keeled back scales giving it a rough appearance. Eyes have round pupils. Belly yellowish. Western individuals have four dark lines along the back, eastern ones have rows of blotches.

Strong, muscular snake that constricts its prey, small mammals and birds. Hunts in warm cloudy weather, often at dusk. Slow-moving, placid, rarely tries to bite even if disturbed. Good climber and swimmer, found in bushes as much as on the ground.

Found along the edges of open woods and hedges, overgrown hillsides, sometimes near marshes or ponds. Not common. Most of Italy (except the north) and Sicily, through much of the Balkans and Greece to the Cyclades. North to western Asia.

Western form (1) occurs in Italy, Sicily, western and south-western Balkans, Greece and the Cyclades. **Eastern Form (2)** occurs in northeastern Greece, eastern Balkans, Turkey. **Young (3)** in both areas have rows of dark spots on back and flanks.

LEOPARD SNAKE

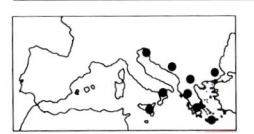

Elaphe situla — up to **100cm**

Medium-sized, fairly slender snake with smooth scales and round pupils. It has deep red to brown, black-edged blotches on its back, and smaller spots on each flank. One large variable blotch at the back of the head often takes the shape of a V.

Usually active by day, sometimes at dusk. Usually ground-living but also climbs well in bushes or among rocks. Some individuals may be aggressive and bite if caught. Non-venomous. Not very fast-moving, constricts its prey, small mammals and birds.

Favours south-facing slopes, screes, dry-stone walls, usually with bushes. Also roadsides, field edges, gardens. Southern Balkans, Greece and Aegean Islands, Crete and Turkey. Southern Italy, eastern Sicily, Malta. East to Asia Minor and Caucasus.

Young have similar pattern to adults. No similar species within its range.

DICE SNAKE
up to **75-100cm**, sometimes longer — *Natrix tessellata*

Medium-sized snake with small narrow head, strongly keeled back scales and round pupils. Colour variable, often grey or olive with an even, regular pattern of dark squarish spots. Belly whitish to yellow or red, and dark-chequered; or almost black.

Aquatic, spending most of its time in water, often submerged for long periods. Crawls or rests on the bottom, but also swims and dives well, coming up for air by exposing the front part of the head; sometimes basks on the bank. Feeds mostly on fish.

Found in clear rivers and streams, ponds and lakes, from sea-level to 1000m. Most of Balkans and Italy (except the south), north to Switzerland in the west and the Ukraine in the east. Isolated populations live on the Rhine in Germany and in Crete.

Dice, Grass and Viperine Snakes are all *Natrix* species, known together as water snakes; this is the most aquatic. **Viperine Snakes** have broader heads, and often dark blotches with light centres on their flanks. **Grass Snakes** are more terrestrial.

VIPERINE SNAKE

Natrix maura — up to **80-100cm**

Rather thickset snake with strongly keeled back scales and round pupils. Usually brown to grey or yellowish, with dark blotches on back and flanks; flank spots may be light-centred. One or two dark ∧ marks on back of head. Belly chequered.

Aquatic. Active by day, often basking on the water's edge, diving if disturbed. Hunts amphibians and fish for food. If cornered, it hisses and strikes but with its mouth closed. It may empty its smelly anal gland if handled. Non-venomous.

Found in or near water, weedy ponds and slow rivers, less often foothill streams or brackish waters near the sea. Also in damp woods and meadows. Iberia, central and southern France to northwest Italy. Balearic Islands, Isles d'Hyeres and Sardinia.

May be mistaken for a viper in colour and behaviour; but many vipers have small, irregular scales on the head and this snake (like other colubrid snakes) has a regular pattern of large, plate-like scales. Vipers also have vertical pupils.

GRASS SNAKE
up to **150cm**, sometimes longer

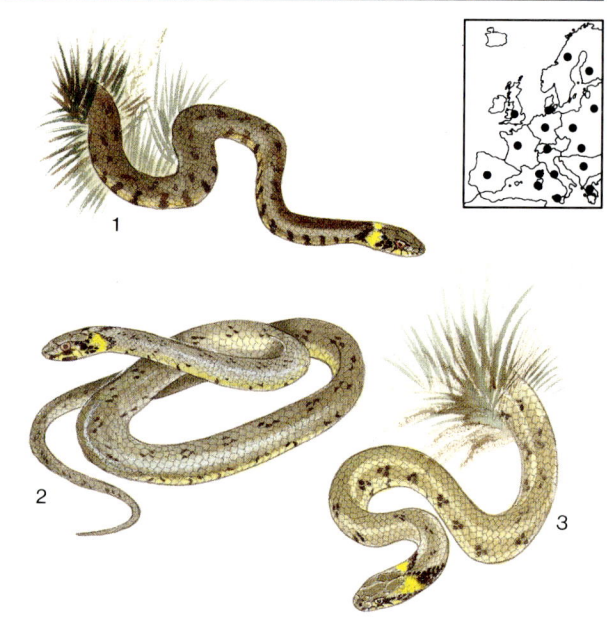

Natrix natrix

Moderately large, often quite thickset snake, with keeled back scales, and round pupils. Colour and pattern variable, but usually two yellow or orange blotches behind the head, followed by dark crescent-shaped marks. Belly chequered white and grey.

Active by day, hunting amphibians for food, often near water. A good swimmer. It may hiss and strike if cornered but does not usually bite. Non-venomous. Empties its smelly anal gland if handled and may feign death, going limp with its mouth open.

Commonest European snake, found in marshes, damp meadows, woods and heaths. Throughout much of Europe, north to central Scand-inavia and Finland, in lowlands in the north, up to 2000m in south. Absent in Scotland, Ireland, Balearic Islands, Crete.

Several subspecies in Europe. **Western Grass Snake** (**1**) occurs in British Isles and western Europe; **Northern Grass Snake** (**2**) in north and east; **Balkan Grass Snake** (**3**) in southeast Europe and northern Italy; Iberian Grass Snake is more uniform in colour.

SMOOTH SNAKE

Coronella austriaca — up to **60-80cm**

Relatively small snake with smooth scales and round pupils. Grey to brown or reddish with dark spots on the back; these may merge into stripes behind the neck. Also a dark stripe on each side of head and neck. Belly more or less uniform.

Rather secretive, burrowing into soil much of the time. Basks in the morning or after rain, avoids hot sun. Slow-moving, creeps away if disturbed, bites if handled. Non-venomous, but may void its smelly anal gland. Hunts mainly lizards for food.

Found in areas with dry loose or sandy soil, often with heather or other vegetation, in open woods, on bushy slopes. Southern England. Across central Europe, north to southern Scandinavia, south to northern Iberia, Italy, Sicily, Balkans and Greece.

Southern Smooth Snake (p.106) is smaller with a yellow to red, often dark-chequered belly. Smooth Snakes are often mistaken for vipers in the south of their range, but have smooth, glossy scales (not keeled ones), and round instead of vertical pupils.

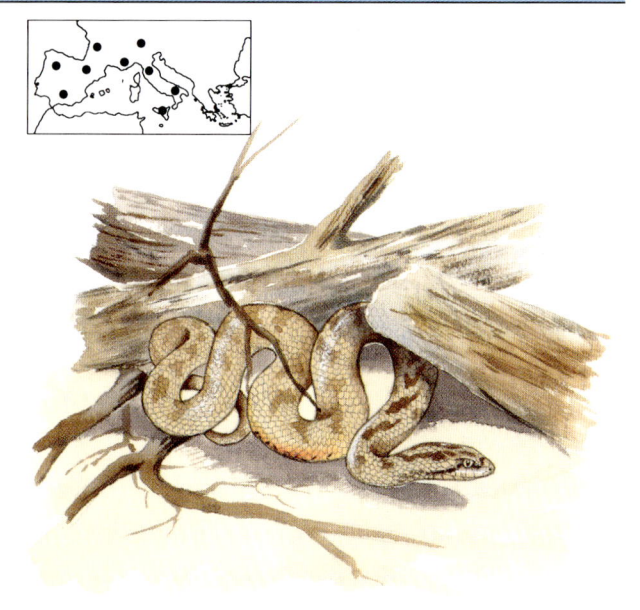

SOUTHERN SMOOTH SNAKE
up to **50-70cm** *Coronella girondica*

Similar to Smooth Snake, but generally smaller and more slender. The dark line on the side of the head does not reach the nostril; the belly is yellow to red with a pattern of dark angular spots or lines.

Another secretive snake, usually emerging at dusk, not by day. Hides by day under stones or piles of logs, in burrows. Slow-moving, non-venomous and not likely to bite. Mostly hunts lizards for food.

Found in a variety of dry places, bushy slopes, fields, edges of woods and hedges, also around stone piles and old walls. At altitudes up to 1500m, across Iberia and southern France to Italy and Sicily. Also in west Austria. Northwest Africa.

Young of **Smooth Snakes** (p.105) and Southern Smooth Snakes both have reddish bellies and are difficult to tell apart. Adult Smooth Snakes have a uniformly coloured belly, a longer line on the side of the head; they are more aggressive and likely to bite.

HOODED SNAKE

Macroprotodon cucullatus — up to **45cm**, sometimes **60cm**

Small snake with smooth scales and flattened head. Light brown with vague dark spots, a dark patch on back of head (the hood) and a dark streak from nostril to mouth. Belly pale yellow to red, usually dark-chequered. Pupils oval in bright light.

Secretive by day; usually active at dusk or by night, hunting lizards. Relatively slow-moving, rears its head if disturbed, and may try to bite. Venom fangs at the back of the mouth contain a mild venom that has no noticeable effect on people.

Found in warm dry stony places with loose soil, in old walls and ruins, scrub and open woods; hiding under rocks, in burrows or buried in the loose soil. In southern Iberia and the Balearic Islands. Also in north Africa.

Sometimes called the False Smooth Snake and a little like a small **Smooth Snake** (p.105). Smooth Snakes are larger and have round pupils in their eyes (note: the pupils of Hooded Snakes can appear to be round in dim light).

CAT SNAKE
usually up to **60-75cm**

Telescopus fallax

Slender snake with smooth scales and broad, flat head. Pupils vertical in bright light, almost round in dim light. Grey to brown with dark patch on head and neck; and rows of dark blotches on body. Belly whitish to pinkish with dark spots.

Often active at dawn and dusk, hiding among rocks by day. They feed mainly on lizards; and have venom fangs at back of mouth. Some will hiss and strike if disturbed. Mouth is too small for fangs to be effective on people, venom causes local swelling.

Found in rocky or stony, often sunny places, bushy slopes, old walls and ruins with bushes. Southern Balkans, Greece and the Greek Islands, including Crete, and north to Italian border on the eastern Adriatic coast. East to southwest Asia. Also Malta.

In Crete, the Cat Snakes are much paler than elsewhere in Europe, pale grey-brown with small pale brown markings that may be entirely absent. Other cat snake species occur in Asia and Africa.

VIPERS

Vipera species

Seven species. The only truly dangerous venomous snakes in Europe. All have recurving venom fangs at the front of the mouth; although slow-moving & often lethargic, many will bite if disturbed & several have highly toxic venom that can kill a man.

They are thickset snakes with a short tail; rough, strongly keeled scales; & a distinct, flattened head, that in many species has small irregular scales on top. Eyes have vertical pupils. Females of all but Blunt-nosed Vipers give birth to live young.

Blunt-nosed Viper
V. lebetina (**1**) is large, up to 150cm long or more, with a flat snout. Very dangerous, bite may be fatal. Found mainly in SW Asia & NW Africa, but also on islands of the western Cyclades, on sunny scrubby hillsides or in ravines, often in a tree.

Ottoman Viper
V. xanthina (**2**) Up to 120cm long with a flat snout (unlike other vipers in its range) & characteristic markings on head. Very dangerous, bite may be fatal. Found around Istanbul. Also much of Middle East, often in farmland or near the coast.

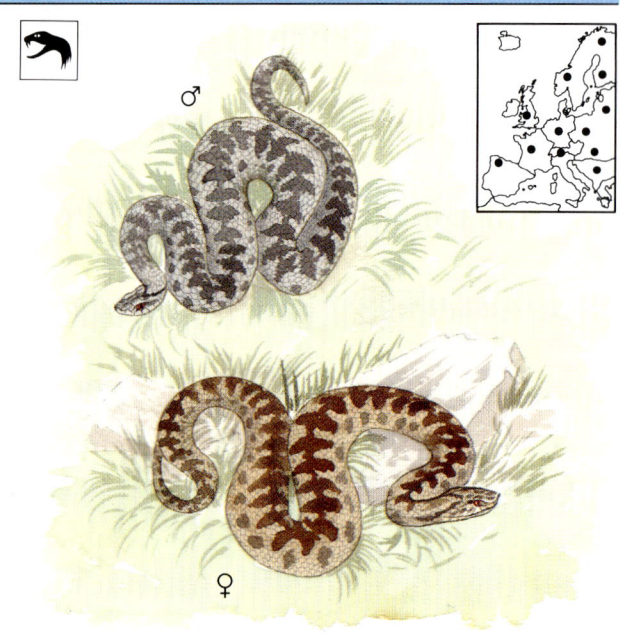

ADDER OR COMMON VIPER
up to **60cm**, sometimes **90cm** *Vipera berus*

A typical viper, but head has several large plate-like scales on top. Snout flat and broad. Males usually pale grey, females browner; both usually have a dark zig-zag stripe on the back. There is usually a V- or X-shaped mark on the back of the head.

Commonest European viper. Usually active by day, ground-living, slow-moving unless disturbed when they may bite hard. They lie in wait for prey (like small mammals) from a hiding place. Bites can be fatal, although fatalities are rare.

Found in a variety of heaths, dunes, grassland, woods, field-edges, more often in mountains in the south. Throughout much of central and northern Europe to the far north. Absent from Ireland, Italy, much of Iberia, Balkans and Mediterranean Islands.

Orsini's Viper (opposite) is smaller, its zigzag back stripe is usually black-edged and it is much less widespread. Adders in northwest Iberia resemble **Asp Viper** (p.112) in colour, have smaller head scales, and may even have a slightly upturned snout.

ORSINI'S VIPER

Vipera ursinii

up to **50-60cm**

The smallest European viper. Head has several large scales on top, as well as small scales. Snout flat and tapering. Body grey to pale brown or yellow, often with darker flanks. On the back there is a dark zigzag stripe, usually edged with black.

Mostly active by day, but may be nocturnal in hot weather. Feeds mostly on insects. Slow-moving, non-aggressive, unlikely to bite unless seriously molested. Less venomous than other vipers, bites cause local pain and swelling but are not fatal.

Isolated montane populations live in mountain meadows in south-eastern France and central Italy. The species is more widely distributed from Austria through Hungary to the western Balkans and east to Asia, in grasslands, open woods or ravines.

Adders (opposite) are more common, larger and the zigzag stripe is not black-edged. **Asp Vipers** (p.112) have an upturned snout.

ASP VIPER
up to **60cm**, sometimes **75cm**

Vipera aspis

More slender than some vipers; the top of the broad triangular head is covered with small scales. The snout is upturned but has no nose-horn. Colour variable, usually with alternating dark crossbars or a wavy, sometimes zigzag, stripe on back.

Active by day in spring and autumn, maybe basking in the sun in the same place; more nocturnal in summer. Slow-moving, ground-living, catches small mammals for food. Not aggressive but will hiss and bite if disturbed; venom dangerous and can be fatal.

Found mostly in warm, dry hills and mountain meadows up to 2000m, most often on rocky limestone slopes. From the Pyrenees north to central France, east to the Black Forest in Germany, south through Italy to Sicily. Also Elba and Montecristo.

Most **Adders** (p.110) have several large scales on top of head, a flat snout and usually a zig-zag pattern on the back; but Iberian Adders are rather different and more like Asp Vipers. **Snub-nosed** and **Nose-horned Vipers** (p.113/4) have a horn on the snout.

SNUB-NOSED VIPER

Vipera latastei — up to **60cm**, sometimes **75cm**

A typical viper with small scales on top of the head. It has an upturned snout usually ending in a nose-horn. Colour usually greyish to brownish with a dark-edged, wavy or zigzag stripe along the back.

Active by day, except in hot weather when it is more nocturnal. Slow-moving, catches small mammals for food. Prone to bite if disturbed, its bite is venomous but not considered dangerous and no human fatalities are recorded.

Found in hills and mountains up to 1300m in Europe, in dry rocky places, open woods and forests. Across Iberia except the extreme north, also in northwest Africa (where it is found at higher altitudes).

Also known as Lataste's Viper. **Asp Vipers** (opposite) and **Adders** (p.110) lack nose-horns, although Asp Vipers have upturned snouts. **Nose-horned Vipers** (p.114) are not found in Iberia or northwest Africa.

113

NOSE-HORNED OR SAND VIPER
usually up to **60-80cm** *Vipera ammodytes*

A typical viper, with small scales on the head. There is a distinct nose-horn on the snout. Usually grey or brown with a dark-edged stripe along the back; this may be a zigzag or formed from a series of more or less joined blotches.

Slow-moving, lethargic but may be active day or night, often climbing into bushes in hot weather and resting in the shade. Hunts small mammals. Hisses if disturbed but unlikely to bite unless molested; but highly venomous, bites can be fatal.

Found in dry rocky places, sunny slopes with scattered bushes, also dry-stone walls; often in mountains in the west and south, also in plains in the east. Northeast Italy, southern Austria and Romania, Balkans, south to the Cyclades. Southwest Asia.

The only snake with a nose-horn on its snout in its range. **Snub-nosed Viper** (p.113) is found in Iberia and northwest Africa.

HERMANN'S TORTOISE
Testudo hermanni — carapace up to **20cm**

Tortoise with strongly domed, sometimes lumpy carapace, brown to yellowish or greenish in colour with varying amounts of dark pigment. It has two plates on the carapace above the tail, a large scale at the tip of its tail, but no spurs on the thighs.

Active mornings and evenings, detected by the constant rustling they make as they move about in the vegetation. Mainly feed on leaves, but will also take carrion, insects etc. Females lay clutches of hard white eggs in loose soil in spring.

Found in meadows and cultivated land, on hillsides, in scrub and woods, dunes with dense vegetation. In warm areas of southern Europe, extreme southern France, western Italy, Balkans and Greece. And many of the Mediterranean Islands.

Spur-thighed Tortoise (p.116) has only one plate on the carapace above the tail, distinct spurs on its thighs, and no scale on the tip of its tail.

GREEK OR SPUR-THIGHED TORTOISE
carapace up to **25cm** *Testudo graeca*

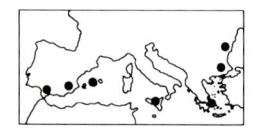

Tortoise with domed, though usually not lumpy, carapace, similar in colour to that of **Hermann's Tortoise** (p.115). Tail has no scale on its tip, there is only one plate on the carapace above the tail, and there are obvious spurs on the thighs.

Active mornings and evenings, feeding on leaves and fruit, also taking snails and worms. They hibernate in burrows in winter, the males fight fiercely in spring before mating, and females lay their hard white eggs in early summer.

Found in dry places, often in scrub, or the slopes of wooded hills up to 1100m in altitude. Southern Spain, the Balearics, southern Italy and Sicily, eastern Balkans, Turkey and some Greek Islands. Also north Africa, Middle East and Asia Minor.

Young Spur-thighed and **Marginated Tortoises** (opposite) can be quite difficult to tell apart where the two species occur together, but they only overlap in Greece.

MARGINATED TORTOISE

Testudo marginata — carapace usually up to **25cm**

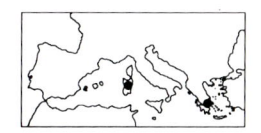

The adult tortoises are distinctive. The carapace is black with a pale orange blotch on each large plate; and it is strongly flared over the tail at the back. There is usually only one carapace plate above the tail.

Mostly active mornings and evenings, taking a siesta midday. They feed on softer shoots of plants and on fruit. Hibernate briefly in winter, emerging in March to mate. Females lay eggs in shallow holes a few weeks later, and young emerge in summer.

Found on dry sunny, rocky or scrub-covered hillsides, often near water, south from Mt Olympos in Greece, on Skyros and Poros and other Greek Islands. Also found on Sardinia, where it is probably introduced.

The young tortoises lack the distinctive colour and flare of the adult carapace; they can be difficult to distinguish from the young of **Spur-thighed Tortoise** (opposite). **Hermann's Tortoise** (p.115) has two carapace plates above the tail.

EUROPEAN POND TERRAPIN
carapace **12-20cm**   *Emys orbicularis*

Terrapin with flattened, more or less oval carapace. Carapace and body dark brown or blackish, usually with yellow spots and streaks. Young are more brightly coloured than adults.

Active by day, hiding in thick vegetation in water or basking at the water's edge, ready to dive at any disturbance. A carnivore, hunting invertebrates, fishes and amphibians. Females lay 4-10 eggs in a hole dug near the water in summer.

Found in slow-moving rivers and stagnant ponds, ditches and marshes, also in brackish water; across southern and much of central Europe. Absent from much of northern France, the British Isles and northern Europe.

Stripe-necked Terrapin (opposite) is lighter in colour, has yellow stripes on the neck; and is found only in Iberia, the southern Balkans and Greece, but also in northwest Africa.

STRIPE-NECKED TERRAPIN
Mauremys caspica — carapace up to **20cm**

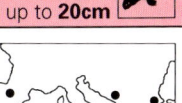

Similar to Pond Terrapin, with the carapace oval and flattened, but lighter in colour, usually greyish brown or olive-green. There are conspicuous yellow stripes on the neck. Young are more brightly coloured, brown with red or yellow markings.

Like the Pond Terrapin, this animal spends its days in water, hiding in water plants or basking at the water's edge but ready to dive. It hunts molluscs, fishes and amphibians. The female lays her eggs in a hole that she digs in the bank in summer.

Found in slow-moving streams, rivers and ponds, also in more open water and swamps; tolerates brackish water well. Found in Iberia, the southern Balkans and Greece. Also in northwest Africa.

Pond Terrapin (opposite) is darker in colour and has no yellow stripes on the neck. It has a much wider range, occurring across southern and much of central Europe.

LOGGERHEAD TURTLE
carapace up to **80-110cm**

Caretta caretta

Marine turtle, with a rather long, heart-shaped, streamlined carapace formed of horny plates. There are five plates on each side. Carapace is red-brown in colour, the broad, scaly flipper-like limbs lighter, the head with dark markings.

Deep water individuals hunt floating jellyfishes, but inshore they take crustaceans, fishes and molluscs as well. Females may lay eggs at night on sandy Mediterranean beaches. Young have a saw-backed appearance and dark streaks on the carapace.

Found in deep water but also near the shore, in the Atlantic and Mediterranean. The commonest turtle in the Mediterranean. They are often caught in fishing nets.

Green Turtle *Chelonia mydas* lives mainly in the tropical Indian, Pacific and Atlantic Oceans, but also drifts north into European Atlantic waters. It is hunted for food (turtle soup). It is brown or olive in colour; the carapace has four plates on each side.

LEATHERY TURTLE

Dermochelys coriacea carapace up to **180cm** (or more)

The largest living turtle and unlike any other. Carapace black, tough and leathery, with a mosaic of small bones embedded in it. There are seven prominent ridges running the length of the carapace. Limbs are heavy flippers without claws.

An oceanic turtle, living out at sea, travelling huge distances in deep water but also seen near the shore in summer. It hunts floating jellyfishes. Now rare and endangered, many have died in fishing nets or in accidents with boats.

Mostly found in tropical seas, but they drift north in the Atlantic Gulf Stream in summer, occasionally as far north as the Arctic. Rarely, a few enter the Mediterranean, where the females may lay eggs at night on a few sandy beaches.

No similar species.

Index and Checklist

Keep a record of your sightings by inserting a tick in the box.

- [ ] ADDER — 110
- [ ] AGAMA, Sling-tailed — 53
- ALGYROIDES,
  - [ ] Dalmatian — 62
  - [ ] Greek — 63
  - [ ] Pygmy — 63
  - [ ] Spanish — 63
- [ ] BOA, Sand — 91
- [ ] CHAMELEON, Mediterranean — 52
- FROG,
  - [ ] Agile — 47
  - [ ] Common — 44
  - [ ] Common Tree — 50
  - [ ] Edible — 49
  - [ ] Iberian — 43
  - [ ] Italian Agile — 47
  - [ ] Marsh — 48
  - [ ] Moor — 45
  - [ ] Painted — 42
  - [ ] Parsley — 33
  - [ ] Pool — 49
  - [ ] Stream — 46
  - [ ] Stripeless Tree — 51
- GECKO,
  - [ ] Kotschy's — 57
  - [ ] Leaf-toed — 56
  - [ ] Moorish — 54
  - [ ] Turkish — 55
- LIZARD,
  - [ ] Balkan Green — 69
  - [ ] Balkan Wall — 77
  - [ ] Bedriaga's Rock — 72
  - [ ] Bocage's Wall — 79
  - [ ] Common Wall — 74
  - [ ] Dalmatian Wall — 80
  - [ ] Erhard's Wall — 78
  - [ ] European Glass — 88
  - [ ] European Worm — 89
  - [ ] Greek Rock — 70
  - [ ] Green — 68
  - [ ] Horvath's Rock — 73
  - [ ] Iberian Rock — 72
  - [ ] Iberian Wall — 75
  - [ ] Ibiza Wall — 79
  - [ ] Italian Wall — 76
  - [ ] Lilford's Wall — 79
- LIZARD (continued),
  - [ ] Maltese Wall — 70
  - [ ] Milos Wall — 81
  - [ ] Mosor Rock — 73
  - [ ] Ocellated — 66
  - [ ] Peloponnese Wall — 81
  - [ ] Sand — 65
  - [ ] Schreiber's Green — 67
  - [ ] Sharp-snouted Rock — 73
  - [ ] Sicilian Wall — 81
  - [ ] Snake-eyed — 64
  - [ ] Spiny-footed — 61
  - [ ] Tyrrhenian Wall — 80
  - [ ] Viviparous — 71
- NEWT,
  - [ ] Alpine — 30
  - [ ] Bosca's — 31
  - [ ] Great Crested — 26
  - [ ] Italian — 32
  - [ ] Marbled — 27
  - [ ] Montandon's — 30
  - [ ] Palmate — 28
  - [ ] Smooth — 29
- [ ] OLM — 18
- RACER,
  - [ ] Algerian Sand — 58
  - [ ] Desert — 60
  - [ ] Spanish Sand — 59
- SALAMANDER,
  - [ ] Alpine — 21
  - [ ] Corsican Brook — 24
  - [ ] Fire — 20
  - [ ] Gold-striped — 25
  - [ ] Italian Cave — 19
  - [ ] Pyrenean Brook — 24
  - [ ] Sardinian Brook — 24
  - [ ] Sardinian Cave — 19
  - [ ] Sharp-ribbed — 23
  - [ ] Spectacled — 22
- SKINK,
  - [ ] Bedriaga's — 83
  - [ ] Greek Legless — 86
  - [ ] Ocellated — 82
  - [ ] Snake-eyed — 84
  - [ ] Three-toed — 85
- [ ] SLOW WORM — 87

SNAKE,
- [ ] Aesculapian — 98
- [ ] Algerian Whip — 92
- [ ] Balkan Whip — 95
- [ ] Cat — 108
- [ ] Dahl's Whip — 96
- [ ] Dice — 102
- [ ] Four-lined — 100
- [ ] Grass — 104
- [ ] Hooded — 107
- [ ] Horseshoe Whip — 92
- [ ] Ladder — 99
- [ ] Large Whip — 94
- [ ] Leopard — 101
- [ ] Montpellier — 97
- [ ] Smooth — 105
- [ ] Southern Smooth — 106
- [ ] Viperine — 103
- [ ] Western Whip — 93
- [ ] Worm — 90

SPADEFOOT,
- [ ] Common — 35
- [ ] Eastern — 35
- [ ] Western — 34

TERRAPIN,
- [ ] European Pond — 118
- [ ] Stripe-necked — 119

TOAD,
- [ ] Common — 36
- [ ] Fire-bellied — 41
- [ ] Green — 38
- [ ] Midwife — 39
- [ ] Natterjack — 37
- [ ] Yellow-bellied — 40

TORTOISE,
- [ ] Greek/Spur-thighed — 116
- [ ] Hermann's — 115
- [ ] Marginated — 117

TURTLE,
- [ ] Leathery — 121
- [ ] Loggerhead — 120

VIPER,
- [ ] Asp — 112
- [ ] Blunt-nosed — 109
- [ ] Nose-horned — 114
- [ ] Orsini's — 111
- [ ] Ottoman — 109
- [ ] Snub-nosed — 113